Church and Nation
in a Secular Age

Church and Nation in a Secular Age

JOHN HABGOOD

Darton, Longman and Todd
London

First published in 1983 by
Darton, Longman and Todd Ltd
89 Lillie Road, London SW6 1UD

ISBN 0 232 51608 1

British Library Cataloguing in Publication Data

Habgood, John
    Church and nation in a secular age.
    1. Church and social problems
    I. Title
    261.1   HN31

    ISBN 0–232–51608–1

Phototypeset by Input Typesetting Ltd, London SW19 8DR
Printed in Great Britain by
Anchor Brendon Ltd
Tiptree, Essex

To my children
Laura, Francis, Ruth and Adrian,
in the hope that when they are
ready to play their full part in
Church and Nation, they will find
both worthy of their glad allegiance.

Contents

Acknowledgements

This book owes its origin to the generosity of my Bishop's Council in suggesting that, after ten years as Bishop of Durham, I should take six months' sabbatical leave. The whole book has had to be planned, researched and written during this period. It was clear to me from the start that if the task could not be completed in six months, it would not be worth attempting it at all. Inevitably, therefore, the book bears the marks of haste, and there are many passages which, given more time, I would prefer to have rewritten. I apologize for them in advance.

I am grateful to the people of the Diocese of Durham for their forbearance in allowing me this time to write, and for keeping their distance even though I was working at home.

Thanks are due to Croom Helm Ltd Publishers for permission to reproduce 'Theological Reflections on Compromise' which first appeared in 1981 in Sims (ed.), *Explorations in Ethics and International Relations*.

I would also like to thank my closest colleagues who have had to carry extra burdens, and especially Michael Ball, Bishop of Jarrow, who with unfailing cheerfulness has managed to do at least two peoples' work, and in whose hands I have been able to leave the diocese with entire confidence.

I am grateful, too, to my wife and family for letting what could have been a holiday be used for a basically unsociable purpose; to my secretary, Maude Harrison, for giving up hours of her time, even at weekends, in typing the manuscript with superb accuracy; to my assistant secretary, Wendy Dunnill, for typing the notes and bibliography, and to Ann Hall for compiling the index.

JOHN HABGOOD
23rd June 1983

Introduction

A bishop should 'speak out', but what can he say?
David Martin in a letter to *The Times*.

The aim of this book can be stated in a single sentence. It is to explore the role of a national church in a secular, pluralist society.

I put it in these general terms because, although inevitably more of my interest lies within the Church of England, the theme has wide implications beyond a particular church in a particular nation. I begin where I am, with the church I know and within which I bear responsibility. But I also recognize from the start that the phrase 'national church', as applied to the Church of England, has for many become increasingly problematic. No discussion of Christianity in Britain can ignore the numerical weakness of all the churches, a weakness in which the Church of England fully shares. Nor can it ignore the fact that much of what is left of the historic national role of the two established churches in England and Scotland, is now exercised in partnership with others, notably through the British Council of Churches.

Question marks can also be put against the phrase 'secular, pluralist society' as a description of present-day Britain. Some, with their eyes on the plight of ethnic minorities, doubt whether we have yet gone very far along the road to becoming truly pluralist. Others might challenge the use of the word 'secular' of a society in which Breakfast Time TV has its own resident astrologer.

My blunt statement of aim, therefore, must be subject to many qualifications. Its main purpose, and the reason why it is couched in sociological jargon, is to indicate a field of interest and to help me to draw some boundaries.

This is not another survey of the past history, present state and future prospects of Christianity in Britain. There has been a spate of such books written in the last decade or so, many of them concentrating specifically on the Church of England,[1] and I see no point in attempting to cover the same ground, even if I were equipped to do so.

Nor is this yet another work on the theology of the church. Here again there is plenty of good material on which to draw, but I propose to take it as read.[2] Readers will find no systematic attempt to go back to biblical roots, no summary of the relationships between church and state, not even much reference to liberation theology which, important though it is in its own context, does not yet seem to me to be easily applicable in Britain.

Though the theme of the book is topical, it has not been chosen just on account of its topicality. Press stories about strained relationships between Lambeth Palace and Downing Street in the aftermath of the Falklands War, recurrent excitements about the appointment of bishops, newspaper articles on the rape of the Book of Common Prayer, and veiled threats of disestablishment from publicity-conscious politicians, are all surface ripples indicating the presence of much deeper currents waiting to be explored. It is these more general issues which are my concern. The topicality of some of their manifestations is a bonus, but not my main reason for writing.

Apart from being expected to 'speak out', a bishop is constantly having to make a wide variety of practical decisions on matters ranging from the closure of old churches and the building of new ones, to settling disputes between parishioners and their clergy; from authorizing an ecumenical experiment to fixing the balance of priorities in his diary. All such decisions imply, among other things, some understanding of the role of the church he serves in relation to the society in which it is set. It may be explicit or implicit, more usually, I suspect, the latter.

1   D. L. Edwards, *Religion and Change* (1969), *The British Churches Turn to the Future* (1973); Leslie Paul, *A Church by Daylight* (1973); Trevor Beeson, *The Church of England in Crisis* (1973); David Sheppard, *Built as a City* (1973); John Adair, *The Becoming Church* (1977); David Perman, *Change and the Churches* (1977); Anthony Russell, *The Clerical Profession* (1980); and others.
2   Richard Niebuhr's *Christ and Culture* (1952) is still probably the best general survey of different ways of being the church. W. H. Vanstone's *Love's Endeavour Love's Expense* (1977), though not specifically about the theology of the church at all, gives a penetrating theological insight into what it actually means to *be* the church.

This is not only true of bishops, who are in any case in danger of over-estimating their importance as spokesmen and decision-makers. Decisions made by individual Christians, and at local church level, do as much, if not more, to determine the character of a church as do those of the designated leaders. The way in which ordinary church members understand the role of their church in relation to society has profound practical implications. Though I write from where I am as a bishop I hope, therefore, that what I say may be seen to have a much wider application. The motivation behind the book is the pressure of actual decision-making. The issues are general and some of the ideas may seem unduly theoretical, but the argument revolves around two key practical questions:

(a) Given the present state of society in Britain, what ought the churches actually be trying to do?
(b) How can the churches minister more effectively to the life of the nation as a whole without thereby sacrificing their integrity?

In terms of method I intend to draw on a source of understanding which I believe has not yet been treated by the churches in this country with the seriousness which it deserves. The sociology of religion suffers neglect in the churches for a variety of reasons, some good, some bad. Straightforward surveys of religious practice, Gallup polls on who believes what, and local investigations designed to answer specific questions for planning purposes, receive on the whole sympathetic attention. It is the more general attempts to convey in sociological terms insights into the function and meaning of religion as a social phenomenon which arouse resistance. Criticisms of barbarous sociological jargon, doubts about the validity of sociological methods, and unease at the implied threat to many traditional religious understandings, all contribute to the denigration of a discipline which, if treated with proper caution, has much to offer and some sharp questions to pose.

When I mentioned to one of my episcopal colleagues what I was intending to do, his immediate retort was, 'You had better hurry up. Departments of sociology are disappearing so rapidly from the universities that there will soon be no sociologists left.' He said it with an air of satisfaction, as one who looked forward to being rid of an irritant. The feelings of sociologists themselves that they are not wanted or listened to by the churches, were expressed forcibly by Dr Homan after he had burnt his fingers over a survey on the use of the Alternative Service Book.[3] David Martin was making the same complaint as long ago as 1967,[4] and there is not much evidence that things have substantially altered since then.

Leslie Paul[5] made valiant efforts to increase the churches' sociological awareness, and Robin Gill[6] in Edinburgh has written a series of books which try to put theology more firmly in its social context, and which explore the interplay between the two disciplines. There are sociologists like Martin himself, Robert Towler and, in the United States, Peter Berger, who write from an explicitly religious standpoint, and whose ideas have penetrated a little way into the consciousness of some clergy and laity, but there seems to be little general awareness within the churches in Britain of sociology as a resource and a challenge which needs to be given proper attention.

Much of my own thinking over the past forty years has been concerned with questions in the broad field of science and religion. It has seemed to me that a faith which ignores one of the most powerful factors in shaping modern consciousness, cannot survive in today's world in anything except an intellectual ghetto. I regard the study of science as an essential part of belief in God as Creator. And I see no future for a Christianity which does not try to come to terms with the best insights science has to offer, while at the same time not allowing itself to be captured and confined by scientific presuppositions. I therefore have an initial predisposition to listen to what the social scientists are saying.

But is sociology really a science? In the hard sense of that word, the answer is probably no. John Ziman, one of the best modern exponents of scientific method from the point of view of a practising scientist, asks whether the behavioural sciences 'can produce a strong, sure, unambiguous framework of concepts and relations as reliable in its own domain as the physical and biological sciences in theirs'.[7] He goes on:

3 Roger Homan, 'Theology and Sociology: A Plea for Sociological Freedom. *Theology*, vol. LXXXIV (1981), pp. 428–38.
4 David Martin, *A Sociology of English Religion* (1967), p. 119.
5 His *The Payment and Deployment of the Clergy* (1964) is, I think, the only national survey ever commissioned directly by the Church of England.
6 *The Social Context of Theology* (1975); *Theology and Social Structure* (1977).
7 John Ziman, *Reliable Knowledge: An Exploration of the Grounds for Belief in Science* (1978), p. 159.

the behavioural sciences are cluttered with innumerable half-articulated speculative models . . . that have never been subjected to critical validation. Standards of theory construction and confirmation have seldom been sufficiently high to distinguish clearly between what is well established, what is essentially conjectural, and what has been thoroughly disconfirmed. Theoretical 'sketches' abound, but there are very few reliable 'maps'. Many of the 'pictures' in the minds of research workers and practitioners are sheer fantasy, contradictory in themselves and having no basis in reality. Such a situation is, of course, deplorable; but it reflects the enormous difficulties of defining consensible observations and discovering consensual theories to explain them.[8]

This is harsh criticism from one whose main discipline is physics. But it is not a totally negative reaction. Only by recognizing the severe limitations of the social sciences, limitations which are inherent in the nature of their subject matter, is it possible to receive in a positive way their genuine and important contribution to human understanding. Ziman summarizes it as follows: 'What we live by in social life is not a series of scientific laws, but *maxims* whose lack of consistency and consensuality is irrelevant to their practical value.'[9]

Sociologists themselves are aware of these limitations. For them the hard facts which form the basis of the natural sciences are scarce and elusive, and the harder they are in mathematical terms the less interesting they frequently become from a sociological perspective. Theorists search for correlations, or try to bring new insights to bear on familiar experiences by describing activities in functional terms which, from the point of view of those performing them, may be interpreted quite differently. Analysis may reveal constraints and tendencies and patterns. David Martin writes of describing 'relationships which make intelligible a wide range of data',[10] but talk of particular activities and responses being 'determined' by social factors always needs to be put in inverted commas. There is no coherent and generally accepted theoretical framework sufficiently strong to give claims to social determinism any plausibility, and none are more conscious of this than those who study the sociology

8   ibid., p. 171.
9   ibid., p. 185.
10 David Martin, *A General Theory of Secularization* (1978), p. 14.

5

of religion. Writers on the subject usually begin by saying that it all depends on one's definition of 'religion', and it only needs a modest acquaintance with the literature to see how different starting-points can lead to widely divergent conclusions.

There is a major distinction between sociologists who stick close to the mathematical analysis of detailed empirical data, and high-level speculative theorists, like Berger, who are trying to answer quite general questions about how human beings construct their social world.[11] The latter provide special temptations for popular-izers, not least because much of the language used has close links with ordinary everyday language, and hence is vulnerable to mis-understanding and misuse. The impenetrable jargon which sociol-ogists are often accused of resorting to only provides a partial defence, since for the most part the jargon consists of ordinary words used in odd and restricted ways. It is therefore easy for an outsider to think he has understood what is being said, when in fact he has missed the point.

I am very conscious myself of the danger of venturing into a realm for which I am not professionally equipped, and I shall no doubt make many mistakes. Nevertheless there comes a point at which those with a practical interest in a subject, who want to use it in ways which are not open to the professionals themselves, have to be prepared to take the risk.

If maxims rather than laws are the fruits of sociological endeav-our, then it should be possible for a sympathetic outsider to gain some enrichment from the subject, without claiming any right to judge between conflicting theories, or to place his own interpret-ations on other people's concepts. So far sociological ideas have not really entered into the bloodstream of the churches to anything like the same extent as the commonplaces of physics and biology. I believe they should. And if they are received in a proper critical spirit, and provided that theology and church history are not assim-ilated into sociology, or vice versa, there is much of value to be learnt.

The behavioural sciences are essentially aids to self-knowledge. Their methods, and the manner of presenting their results, can appear to many Christians as dehumanizing. To reduce individuals to statistics, and to look for the 'determinants' of spiritual move-

11   Peter L. Berger, *The Social Reality of Religion* (1969).

ments in social forces, offends against deeply held religious views about the way God works. To claim that what is being done is only an extension of what has already been done to our self-understanding by physics, chemistry, biology and psychology, is only to make matters worse, since the realm of communal and interpersonal relationships has been for many a last line of defence against the encroachment of science. But just as a knowledge of the other sciences can in the long run be liberating rather than threatening, so I believe sociological self-knowledge, such as it is, can bring real liberation. At its most profound, self-knowledge frees us from the tyranny of our own preconceptions. And that, as I shall argue later, is a step on the road to God.

In the meantime, let me try to justify these claims about the value of sociology at a much more mundane level. *Churches and Churchgoers* is a study of patterns of church membership in some fifteen or so denominations in the British Isles in the period between 1700 and 1970.[12] The statistics are mostly derived from the churches themselves, and reveal highly instructive patterns of growth and decline. Short-term cyclical variations in membership, interpreted within the churches as periods of revival and decay, are linked by the authors with a two-stage process of becoming a church member. On their interpretation, members are usually made from what they call 'adherents', a less tightly-knit group who acknowledge a relationship with a particular church without being committed to it. When the church is in an active phase there is an initial high recruitment rate from adherence to membership, while new adherents are themselves recruited much more slowly. The pool of adherents thus decreases, recruitment to membership drops, and a combination of falling growth and high losses weakens faith in the revival which then passes into a declining phase.

The authors' interpretation is a good deal more subtle than my summary of it in a sentence or two might suggest. I quote it as an interesting small-scale example of how a sociological explanation can illuminate a familiar experience in church life without devaluing the spiritual experiences and efforts of those actually involved.

Even more striking are the large-scale cyclical variations which reveal an astonishing degree of congruence between the different

12   Robert Currie, Alan Gilbert and Lee Horsley, *Churches and Churchgoers: Patterns of Church Growth in the British Isles since 1700* (1977).

denominations. Since it is unreasonable to suppose that all the churches studied during the period in question were subject to the same internal influences on their patterns of growth and decline, the authors look for what they call 'exogenous factors', in other words factors operative in the wider context of Britain as a whole. Obvious reference points are the two wars in this century, both accompanied by religious decline and followed by periods of growth. But the resemblances between the churches go deeper than this, and the statistics frequently match each other in quite fine detail. There is even a very close inverse relationship between membership of the major Protestant churches and of the Rationalist Press Association;[13] since one is numbered in millions and the other in thousands there can be no question of explaining this in terms of an actual transference of membership.

The authors conclude that exogenous factors, by which they mean such general tendencies as secularization, together with economic and political changes, are a major element in the growth or decline of the churches. 'Indeed it seems probable', they say, 'that, whatever efforts are expended by a church, increased recruitment cannot be obtained in unfavourable exogenous conditions.'[14]

Such a generalization has to be set against observations from the direct experience of anybody who has to deal with more than a single local church. It is clear that personalities do in fact make a tremendous difference, that an individual church may grow or shrink for reasons which are plainly connected with the way its members behave, and that effort, though frustrated in difficult times, is not necessarily wasted. All this may be true on the small scale, but it may also be liberating to realize that difficult times are related to factors outside the control of particular individuals and congregations, and that there is therefore no need to feel guilty about them.

For those who try to look at the larger strategies of church life the kind of patterns revealed in *Churches and Churchgoers* have an obvious relevance, though it would be foolish to rush to the conclusion that church policies make no difference.

I have quoted this study at some length as an example of how a fairly straightforward statistical exercise, on material already avail-

13   ibid., p. 102.
14   ibid., p. 98.

able in church files, can produce some surprising results with considerable practical implications. These will be considered further in chapter 5. My main purpose at present is to justify the use of sociological material for the benefit of those who are suspicious of it, or who doubt its relevance in a church context where theology and spiritual discernment ought to take precedence over the speculative theories of those who count heads, or interpret questionnaires, or generalize from history. I take the point being made by such critics, but would simply repeat that Christians ought not to refuse any legitimate road to knowledge, especially knowledge of themselves. And if the mirror held up to the churches sometimes shows an unflattering picture, that in itself may be good for the soul. Furthermore despite the fact that the sociology of religion has suffered a series of crises about its own identity, it can in practice provide illumination, as I hope the following pages will demonstrate.

There remains a more radical objection to what I am attempting in this book. Dr Edward Norman has made himself notorious as a twister of bishops' tails, and part of his charge against them is that they have capitulated too easily 'to the inflated system of social workers, psychologists, sociologists, educationalists, liberal windbags and chattering clergymen stuffed full of bourgeois values'.[15] *Church and Society in England*[16] is an important and perceptive survey of two hundred years of episcopal utterances, which rams home the point again and again that church leaders have been too readily attracted by the fashionable thinking of their day, and have therefore constantly reflected secular rather than Christian values. This subservience to the secular has been compounded by the class interests of church leaders, which have led them to relate more easily to the 'liberal intelligentsia' than to their own people. The Church is thus doubly divided; within itself by a leadership out of touch with the ordinary people it should be serving; and divided from its own roots in a transcendent gospel which, if it is taken seriously, shows up the relativity of all merely human judgements and political manoeuvrings.

Despite the extravagance and partiality with which many of his

15 M. Cowling, *Religion and Public Doctrine in Modern England* (1980), p. 444.
16 E. R. Norman, *Church and Society in England 1770–1970. A Historical Study* (1976).

9

points are made, there is an important core of truth in Norman's main thesis, enough at least to make a bishop setting out to expound some sociological ideas, pause in his tracks and ask himself what he is doing. My difficulty is focused in Norman's repeated use of the word intelligentsia. Presumably he is not decrying the importance of sound scholarship, or he would not himself be attempting to write scholarly history. I have not in fact noted him including historians in his lists of 'liberal windbags', though his colleague at Peterhouse, Maurice Cowling, does precisely that in a huge volume which demonstrates the infection of liberal thinking in the Cambridge History Faculty.[17] Perhaps history is the discipline *par excellence* which shows up the frailty of human efforts to transcend one's own times.

But might not sociology make a similar claim? In searching for patterns and trends, and in making unfamiliar categorizations, it can provide a fresh perspective. In particular, if one of the defects of church leadership is that it is out of touch with its own constituency, then perhaps there is something to be learnt from those who have taken the trouble to study in some detail how the mass of people actually behave and what they say they believe. If such investigators are dismissed as part of the liberal intelligentsia, then I wonder where one is supposed to draw the line, and how anybody looking for enlightenment in disciplines other than his own can avoid Dr Norman's strictures. I grant the importance of the distinction between good scholars and bad scholars. I acknowledge the need to expose the presuppositions underlying branches of study, especially those which touch closely on human life. But I suspect that the effective definition of 'liberal intelligentsia' depends on where one stands, and if one stands to the left of Dr Norman one is classified as part of it.

Before leaving the subject of the class interests of bishops, it may be worth noting a small point of some educational significance. In a classic experiment performed in 1949[18] it was observed that better educated people tend to be more influenced by a two-sided presentation of a case, whereas the less well educated are more influenced by a one-sided approach. A possible explanation is that education provides the skill needed to handle conflicting informa-

17 M. Cowling, op. cit.
18 Cited in Peter Kelvin, *The Bases of Social Behaviour: An Approach in Terms of Order and Value* (1969), p. 63.

tion, as well as an attitude of mind more resistant to being taken in. If this is true, one might expect to find leaders in touch with the more educated elements in society being forced, simply by the need to communicate effectively, into a balanced liberal style, which is then interpreted as threatening or ineffective by those at the other end of the educational scale. I mention this, not in order to deny the significance of the valid points made by Norman about the class orientation of bishops, but as a reminder that there are other dimensions to the problem.

It is this sense that there is always more to be said, and a hundred different qualifications to be made, which creates such difficulties for the behavioural scientists, and for those who would discover some clues from them about how to answer urgent practical questions. Somehow one has to listen to experts without expecting too much from them, or being inhibited by them, or being captured by their presuppositions, and what one hears then has to be related to what one knows in one's own experience. In a word, one has to do the best one can with what is available. Monica Furlong wrote:

> In a world of experts everyone becomes afraid to know anything, even the things they do know. Knowledge becomes something hard-edged; we have lost the awareness that even the most sober fact is ambivalent and uncertain.[19]

The first part of this book, comprising chapters 1 to 4, is mainly theoretical, and I rely heavily on the published literature. In chapter 1 I explore ambiguities in the concept of secularization, and conclude that some of the sweeping claims made about Britain now being a secular society need very careful interpretation. Chapter 2 centres on the questions – What is it that holds pluralist societies together? And what part does or should religion play in this? Chapter 3 looks at the concept of privatization and asks how far the churches are still justified in adopting a public role, especially in matters of political controversy. This leads on to some theological reflections about the nature of the church in chapter 4, and the need to hold in tension the stabilizing role envisaged in chapter 2, and the more prophetic role envisaged in chapter 3.

The remaining chapters are mainly practical and relate much more directly to my own experience. If the selection of topics seems

19   Monica Furlong, *Travelling In* (1971), p. 58.

arbitrary and incomplete, this is because the principle of selection has been personal involvement. The topics are intended as illustrations of the general theme of the book, not as a definitive list of the most important issues facing the churches.

No bishop can ignore the phenomenon of folk religion which sometimes impinges on him even more closely than on the parochial clergy. Nor can he be unconscious of his position as part of the establishment. I have had experience as a member of the House of Lords for ten years, and of the General Synod for the same length of time. The latter is included as a topic, because it often appears as a convenient target for criticism of the Church of England at parish level and in Parliament and beyond. Much of this criticism has centred on the subject of liturgical change, and as chairman of the committee which devised and brought to completion the Alternative Service Book 1980, I have felt the sharp end of it. Ecumenism has been one of my constant concerns since the early 1960s, and I had a large hand in founding, and was subsequently principal of, the only ecumenical theological college serving the main-stream churches in England. More recently I was a member of the ill-fated Churches' Council on Covenanting, and have done work both for the British Council of Churches and for the World Council of Churches.

Chapter 10 on the nuclear weapons' issue, may seem the odd one out in a list which is otherwise heavily ecclesiastical. I include it partly as a reminder that the most important issues facing our society are not ecclesiastical ones. It also provides a useful example of the interrelationship between ethical and political thinking. In addition it fulfils my criterion of personal involvement since, as the British President of an international body which brings together Christians in a variety of relevant disciplines to discuss defence and disarmament questions,[20] I have had unusual opportunities to learn about the subject from experts.

The appendix on Compromise was originally published in a book of essays[21] written in honour of a Quaker friend and colleague, Sydney Bailey, himself a notable expert in matters of defence and disarmament, and a prime example of a Christian who is both

20 Council on Christian Approaches to Defense and Disarmament, usually known as C.C.A.D.D.
21 Nicholas A. Sims (ed.), *Explorations in Ethics and International Relations* (1981).

informed and effective within the political sphere. Its theme bears a close relationship to some of the themes of this book, but I decided not to try to rewrite it for inclusion in the main text.

A good deal of what appears in the second half of the book may seem unduly preoccupied with the domestic affairs of the Church of England. Let me repeat that this is not through lack of concern for other churches and other faiths, or indeed for other parts of Britain besides England. I think it best, however, to treat them tangentially, on the principle that one should centre one's thoughts on what one knows, in the hope that any illumination which results will benefit others as well. If it is true that all the religious bodies in this country are having to operate under the same kind of social pressures, to concentrate for illustrative purposes on one of them may help to give a huge subject some coherence.

1

A Secular Society?

In the Autumn of 1981 I visited several countries in the Middle East as a member of a small delegation to the Middle East Council of Churches.[1] On our first evening in Beirut, at a briefing session with our hosts, we were initiated into the extraordinary complexities of Lebanese politics. There was much talk of the P.L.O., of Syria and Israel, and of deep social and religious divisions, not least in Lebanon itself. But the most pressing concern, and one which surfaced again and again throughout our visit, was summed up in the question – How can the Middle East develop a tolerant religious humanism, of a kind which might enable warring religious groups to live together in peace, without forfeiting the strength of its ancient religious culture? Or to put it in different words – Is it possible to reap the benefits of modernization without its attendant disadvantage, secularization?

Lebanon feels the full force of these questions. Until the recent disasters it was one of the main points of contact between the Arab world and the West. It is also a prime example of a country in which religious affiliation determines all the most important aspects of social life. For a first-time visitor the contrast with Western society is startling. Yet the very fervour with which the issue of Western influence is discussed, and the violence of the extremist reactions against it, is a measure of the fear underlying the questions. The fact that Israel, as the only truly modern state in the area, also shows symptoms of secularization, adds a further religious twist to the spiral of political mistrust.

It is easier to use the word 'secularization', though, than to know precisely what it means. From a Middle Eastern perspective it is a

1 An account of the visit is to be found in *Towards Understanding the Arab/Israeli Conflict* (British Council of Churches, 1982).

convenient label for what they see as the loss of an all-important religious dimension to life. An Australian sociologist, Glasner, in criticizing the concept refers to it as 'an all-purpose explanation for many of the supposed ills of contemporary society'.[2] Wilson, starting from a definition of religion in terms of church activities, charts the statistics of decline in Britain, and describes secularization in terms of the loss of 'social significance' for religion.[3] Martin, on the other hand, using a broad historical and international approach, repeatedly stresses the ambiguity of the concept, and is more concerned to describe the ways in which religion expresses itself in different social contexts than to identify a single secularizing process.[4] Chadwick, writing about the changes in the European mind in the nineteenth century, highlights the ambiguities and uncertainties, but concludes that something radical happened: 'I do not think it an abuse of such a term to call this radical process, still in part so obscure to the enquirer, still in part undefined and possibly in part undefinable, by the name of secularization . . .'[5]

It all depends on where one stands and what one believes religion to be. There are clear contrasts between Middle Eastern and Western societies, as there are between the Middle Ages in Europe and today, though whether all the religious losses in the process of modernization are on one side is open to question.

> You'll say, once all believed, man, woman, child,
> In that dear middle-age these noodles praise.
> How you'd exult if I could put you back
> Six hundred years, blot out cosmogeny, geology,
> Ethnology, what not,
> (Greek endings with the little passing-bell
> That signifies some faith's about to die)
> And set you square with Genesis again, –
> When such a traveller told you his last news,
> He saw the ark a-top of Ararat
> But did not climb there since 'twas getting dusk
> And robber bands infest the mountain's foot!

2 P. E. Glasner, *The Sociology of Secularization: A Critique of a Concept* (1977), p. 10.
3 Bryan Wilson, *Religion in Secular Society* (1966).
4 Martin, *A General Theory of Secularization*.
5 Owen Chadwick, *The Secularization of the European Mind in the Nineteenth Century* (1975), p. 265.

15

How should you feel, I ask, in such an age,
How act? As other people felt and did;
With soul more blank than this decanter's knob,
Believe – and yet lie, kill, rob, fornicate
Full in belief's face, like the beast you'd be![6]

Even the contrast between so-called primitive religion and religion in modern societies is not as clear-cut as it is often thought to be. In a frequently quoted passage the anthropologist, Mary Douglas, questions the notion that there is some primitive religious baseline from which the process of decline can be measured.

> Secularization is often treated as a modern trend, attributable to the growth of cities or to the prestige of science, or just to the breakdown of social forms. But we shall see that it is an age-old cosmological type, a product of definable social experience, which need have nothing to do with urban life or modern science. Here it would seem that anthropology has failed to hold up the right reflecting mirror to contemporary man. The contrast of secular with religious has nothing whatever to do with the contrast of modern with traditional or primitive. The idea that primitive man is by nature deeply religious is nonsense. The truth is that all the varieties of scepticism, materialism and spiritual fervour are to be found in the range of tribal societies.[7]

She sees the character of tribal religion as related, not to the primitiveness or otherwise of the tribe, but to the characteristic types of relationship within it and to the degree of articulation of social roles. Where there are close face-to-face relationships and clearly defined roles, one would expect to find a strong ritual piety. Where relationships are much looser and people move freely in 'an uncharted, and unsystematized, unbounded social world'[8] the development of an ordered, sacramental type of religion becomes impossible. To this extent there are close resemblances between irreligious pygmy tribes and modern, loosely structured families where everybody 'does their own thing'.[9]

A corollary of this view is that the shift from a close-knit village culture to a more diffuse and anonymous city culture, by distancing

6 Robert Browning, *Bishop Blougram's Apology.*
7 Mary Douglas, *Natural Symbols* (Penguin edn, 1970), p. 36.
8 ibid., p. 34.
9 ibid., p. 55.

relationships and destroying roles, is likely to diminish religious practice. In this indirect way her analysis supports the theory that secularization is somehow linked with the process of modernization, but it undermines the notion that this is a straight-line historical progression from some high state of primitive religious observance to modern irreligion.

It is open to doubt how far in any age the majority of people have been 'really religious'. There have been periods of church domination in Europe, periods when for virtually everybody the main forms of activity and expression have had a religious flavour. But how much, asks Glasner, do we really know, for example, about Tudor popular religion and its relation to witchcraft?[10] How far in a given society do religious ideas penetrate, and what is the relationship between this penetration and literacy, powers of abstraction, forms of education and art? Gay's work on the geography of religion in England shows striking differences of religious observance in different areas, and illustrates the length of time it must have taken for religious changes to percolate from the centre to the more remote regions. A map of the distribution of Roman Catholics in 1603, for instance, shows that the numbers varied almost in proportion to their distance from London, with the populations of Durham and Northumberland still remaining more than 75 per cent Roman Catholic over forty years after the Elizabethan Settlement.[11] Nearly four centuries later the North-east still has a distinctive pattern of religious allegiance.

Weber distinguished between 'heroic religiosity' and 'the religion of the mass', and Dostoievsky hit a sensitive spot in his parable of the Grand Inquisitor. It is the few who have to carry the religious burdens of the many, and their understanding of religion may be quite different from that of their followers.

> All will be happy, all the millions of creatures except the hundred thousand who rule over them. For only we, we who guard the mystery, shall be unhappy. There will be thousands of millions of happy babes, and a hundred thousand sufferers who have taken upon themselves the curse of the knowledge of good and evil.[12]

10 Glasner, p. 71.
11 John D. Gay, *The Geography of Religion in England* (1971), p. 276.
12 F. Dostoievsky, *The Brothers Karamazov* (Everyman edn), vol. I, p. 226.

Give or take a good deal for Dostoievskian exaggeration, but the point is surely indisputable that the so-called 'high' periods of religion may not have been all they seemed on the surface. Whichever way one looks at them, religious changes are hard to identify and assess. Nevertheless, in Chadwick's words, in the last two centuries or so 'something happened' to European religion. What was it?

One type of change, which is obvious even on the most superficial account, is what the sociologists call 'structural differentiation'. A major characteristic of modern societies is the extent to which functions become specialized and rationalized. The old omni-competent agencies, Crown and Church, which once dominated almost every aspect of life, give place to a multitude of specialist bodies each with its own relative autonomy, and each removing from the earlier bodies some part of their former significance. Anthony Russell documents the process insofar as it applies to one small area of church life in the nineteenth century through the changing role of the clergy.[13] He illustrates how a role which was once fully integrated into the society it served, and touched ordinary life at numerous points, not only as pastor and leader of worship, but as clerk, law officer, almoner, teacher, officer of health and politician, became progressively restricted and professionalized as other professions took over its former functions. This was all part of the process, repeatedly described by sociologists of religion, whereby the former pervasive influence of religion, seen as legitimating the social order, has been channelled into one specialized activity among others. It is only a short step from here to seeing this specialized activity as a minority interest, which has less and less significance for the life of society as a whole, and belongs primarily to the realm of private choice.

The effects of this process in Britain are all too evident. The story has been well told by Gilbert,[14] among others, and for my purposes there is no point in trying to summarize it. City and suburban life in Britain are not now, and probably never have been, centred around the churches, and in country areas the churches count for a great deal less than used to be the case. The historic forms of institutional religion have declined, and this decline is one of the

13 Russell, *The Clerical Profession*.
14 Alan D. Gilbert, *The Making of Post-Christian Britain* (1980).

symptoms of the modern differentiation of society, which is itself inherent in the transition to a complex urban culture. Such facts are too well-known to need documentation.

The interpretation of their significance for religion varies considerably. Those who see religion primarily in institutional terms, as measured by the statistics of church attendance, are apt to lose interest in bodies which now seem to consist very largely of minority groups of elderly women. Attention focuses on the more spectacular phenomena of the sects whose growth and vigour is contrasted unfavourably with the staid and moribund representatives of the old order, and there is no shortage of advocates to point the main-line churches in a more sectarian direction.

Those who take a more functionalist view of religion, following Durkheim, ask how the role previously fulfilled by the churches in maintaining social cohesion is now provided by other means. This will form the theme of the next chapter. To ask the question is by implication to define religion in a much broader way than in the previous paragraph. Morris Cohen, in writing about 'baseball as a national religion',[15] was no doubt being partly frivolous, but I have enough personal experience of the effects of Sunderland's football performance on the morale of the town to know that there is at least a quasi-religious dimension to what at first sight might seem to be a thoroughly secular activity. On a Durkheimian view, all integrating value-systems, from 'the American way of life' to the most formal of civic ceremonies, are by definition religious.

Some interpreters of the process of structural differentiation see it as bringing positive religious gain. What is taking place is not an overall decline in religion; indeed there is no firm starting-point from which such a decline might be measured. We are witnessing a redefinition of the role of religion in society, which is freeing it for the better performance of its primary function. This has nothing to do with being the cement of society, but is about the search for personal meaning. The nineteenth-century view that Christianity was essential for the maintenance of the moral unity of society, and as a means of justifying unselfish behaviour, has, on this interpretation, given way to a much more complex system of social justifications reflecting the many separate concerns which now constitute

15   Morris R. Cohen, *The Faith of a Liberal*, cited in L. Schneider (ed.), *Religion, Culture and Society* (1964), p. 334.

a modern society. Socially powerless churches, ministering to individuals and no longer having to worry about broader social functions, can be better embodiments of universal social ideals, just as a monarchy, stripped of constitutional powers, can be a better symbol of unity. Let the Church be the Church is the aim, and the means are to hand in the removal of religion from its public frame. Luckmann puts it thus:

> The contemporary marginalization of church religion and its 'inner secularization' appear as *one* aspect of a complex process in which the long-range consequences of institutional specialization of religion and the global transformations of the social order play a decisive role. What are usually taken as the symptoms of the decline of traditional Christianity may be symptoms of a more revolutionary change: the replacement of the institutional specialization of religion by a new social form of religion.[16]

This 'new social form' must inevitably be more private and more diversified. In fact diversification within religion, as well as differentiation between religion and other social functions, is seen as one of the main symptoms of secularization, and is on the whole regarded as a strength rather than a weakness from the sociological perspective. The point will be considered further in chapter 9.

Meanwhile, as a further illustration of the significance of structural differentiation, particularly as it applies to the relationship between churches, it is worth noting the extent to which social change in Britain during the nineteenth century was eased and kept within bounds by the fact that political conflict could find a religious expression. The struggle between the Established Church and Dissent may not have helped religion very much, but it provided a framework within which all sorts of other interests, of a potentially more destructive kind, could be pursued without the risk of social breakdown. Wilson comments that 'religious toleration came sooner and extended further throughout the social structure than political toleration',[17] the implication being that the former helped to prepare the way for the latter.

A much more comprehensive study of the relationship between religious allegiance and social stability has been pioneered by David

16 T. Luckmann, *The Invisible Religion* (1967), p. 90.
17 B. Wilson, p. 99.

Martin.[18] He ranges widely around the Christian world using as one of his indicators the balance between the Catholic and Protestant elements in a given society. Catholicism, he says, is by nature monopolistic, so wherever it dominates within a particular nation there is bound sooner or later to be conflict with the monopolistic tendencies of the State. He classifies countries by their resilience in coping with revolutionary change, and concludes that in Catholic countries religion tends to share in the polarizations of society; Catholicism, for example, frequently breeds anti-clericalism. Countries with a mixed religious tradition tend to absorb their divergencies, as in England where the distribution of religious allegiance facilitated moderate politics while at the same time excluding extreme secularism. The Catholic minority in England tends to be allied with the moderate left, where it helps to counterbalance the Church of England which, by collusion with upper-class styles, 'prevents religion crossing the status divide to the majority of the working class'.[19] Where it has a monopoly the Roman Catholic Church stands officially on the political right though, as is clear from Central and Southern America, there are political conditions which can shift at least some elements away from this traditional stance.

Martin's theory is lengthy and subtle, and such a crude summary cannot possibly do justice to it. The main point to note at the moment, however, is the positive evaluation given to a balanced religious diversity.

Sociologists of religion love to analyse the religious scene in the United States, not only because many of them are American, but because the United States represents balanced religious diversity in its purest form. A country which was from the start deliberately designed to be secular and which allows no public national expressions of religion, has nevertheless managed to develop a strong enough concensus to hold itself together, and maintains a much higher level of religious practice than in any of the older parts of Christendom, with the exception of Poland.

What is even more striking is that the country which has gone furthest in the direction of modernization, and the secularization which is claimed to accompany it, still retains this strong hold on

18   Martin, *A General Theory of Secularization.*
19   ibid., p. 32.

religion. Many explanations are given. Herberg in a classic study argued that in a huge, diverse, melting-pot of a nation, Americans find their identity in religion.[20] Others refer to a kind of 'religion in general', over and above its manifestations in particular denominational allegiances, which is part of the American way of life. There is also the civic religion of the Flag and the Constitution. And unkind critics have even suggested that so-called 'religious' Americans may not be so religious after all, but that secularism instead of isolating the churches has come right inside them. Whatever the explanation, the United States provides yet another example of the complexities which have to be borne in mind when speaking of á 'secular society'.

As well as the structural differentiation of institutions, there is also the secularization of the mind, and to this we must now turn. In many ways it is more fundamental than the social changes just considered, and is even more elusive to pin down precisely. Religious habits of thought, language, conventions have changed out of all recognition in Britain in the last few centuries. But what has been the internal significance of these changes? What differences of religious quality are entailed? Chadwick warns against exaggerating the element of 'disenchantment', which was the word used by Weber in first describing the process of secularization. He adds – 'We may have less sense of providence in our lives.'[21] The First World War contributed to this process of 'distancing God from the detail of human disaster'. Elsewhere he refers to the axiom 'miracles do not happen' as lying near the heart of the shift in attitude he is trying to define. It is all bound up, too, with a sweeping rejection of authority, which can easily become the ultimate recipe for sterile scepticism.

Gilbert refers to a narrowing of consciousness. Religion is no longer attacked, but ignored. 'The crisis of contemporary Christianity lies not in challenges to the truth of its dogmas, but the fact that people in a secular culture have become increasingly "tone-deaf" to any orchestration of these dogmas.'[22]

Such losses in capacity, or subtle changes in consciousness, are not the same as straightforward loss of belief in the supernatural. In fact a remarkable number of people seem to have no difficulty

20 W. Herberg, *Protestant, Catholic, Jew* (1960).
21 Chadwick, pp. 258, 262, 17.
22 Gilbert, p. 13.

in believing in the supernatural, whether in the form of witchcraft or astrology or some pseudo-scientific mythology, but have no means of relating this to official theologies, or indeed of seeing any point in official theologies as somehow exploring matters of primary human concern.

One way of categorizing these changes is as a direct cultural inheritance from the Enlightenment. Langdon Gilkey in an influential essay has described how

The Enlightenment saw itself as representing a new era for human history on three major grounds:

(a) Correct, cumulative and fruitful methods of knowing had been discovered and developed; with science 'we now know how to know', and through that expanding knowledge we can count on an increasing control over the various natural forces threatening human welfare.

(b) The practical application of this new and expanding knowledge of 'causes' in an expanding technology – and through that in an expanding industrialism – would provide the unquestioned blessing of a plethora of goods for general consumption. With the banishing of ignorance, poverty could also be banished.

(c) The curse of traditional superstition and of unexamined authority (especially in religion) could now be eradicated, making rational structures possible (for the first time in history) in the political, legal, social and moral domains.[23]

His next sentence is, 'Our century has seen each of these grounds for optimism radically questioned, if not shattered . . .'

Despite the radical questioning, however, and despite the horrors of the twentieth century and the disenchantment with philosophies of progress, the influence of Enlightenment thinking remains embedded in many of the structures and assumptions of ordinary life. People who may never have heard of the Enlightenment, and who know little of science and its works, and who might even be sceptical of some large-scale claim about 'progress', nevertheless act on the assumption that things ought to get better and better, and that human effort is the key to their improvement. And there are solid grounds for doing so. Life for huge numbers of people has been

23 Langdon Gilkey, 'The New Watershed in Theology' in *Soundings*, vol. LXIV (1981), pp. 119–120.

eased and enlarged, and the agents of that improvement – science, industrialization and the rational bureaucratic organization of human affairs – have been accepted, despite their darker aspects, and have overshadowed the seemingly more marginal experiences which give rise to religious questioning. In a secure world where poverty is the concern of the State, where disease is being conquered and death can be sanitized, why bother about the residual reminders of human vulnerability and mortality? Still less, why bother about sin?

For the majority of people shifts in consciousness are mediated, not through the interplay of ideas, but through the unexamined assumptions by which life is lived. The secularization of the mind, therefore, while at one level it has an important intellectual dimension, is much more than an intellectual phenomenon. People cannot be argued into belief, or argued out of it, if all the circumstances of their lives point in the opposite direction.

There are in fact various levels of unbelief, and evangelism as commonly understood only deals with the most superficial of them. Traditional evangelism is about encouraging deeper commitment on the part of those who already feel themselves as belonging, even if faithlessly, within a religious world of discourse. Beyond these are the millions who appear to have little access to such a world of discourse, who have no meaningful language for religion, and whose perceptions have been shaped by environments in which religion has no place.

The point must not be exaggerated. The secularization of the mind has its limits, as will be spelt out more fully in chapter 5. Science and technology can generate their own mythologies, and the growth of the cults and other bizarre manifestations, including the various counter-culture movements, are signs that some limits of secularization have been reached. One possible explanation for the attraction of mass movements like C.N.D. is that they allow middle-class people to tap some religious resources, and even use religio-moral language, in a secular cause, which is all the more powerful for centring on the deep emotional issue of security.[24] Religion is by no means dead. It is its association with official theology which is suspect, for reasons bound up with anti-authoritarianism, as well as with the inaccessibility of traditional religious

24   Martin, *A General Theory of Secularization*, p. 64.

language, and for broad social reasons which must now be considered in a little more detail.

Peter Berger[25] has been one of the main protagonists of Weber's view that modernization is 'carried' into contemporary consciousness via the institutional framework of a modern technologically based society. The claim is that the very conditions of technological production, and the bureaucratic organization of society, in themselves have a deep influence on the way in which people living in that society think and feel, whether or not they are directly involved in industrial or bureaucratic activity.

Technological production, for instance, separates the world of work from private life, and then imposes its own standards on the former, whereby human relations become subordinate to technical requirements. Just as machines consist of components made and controlled by rational processes, so those who operate them begin to share a similar apprehension of reality, and are themselves dealt with by a species of 'social' engineering.

Bureaucracy has even more pervasive effects in that it touches most people's lives at an increasing number of points, and conveys something of its own values to them in so doing. The stress on order, competence, proper procedures, referral to higher authorities, anonymity and impersonality, all essential concomitants of efficiency and fairness, can in fact add up to give a devastating impression of some faceless machine. The main message is that the world is potentially organizable, that its business can best be conducted by strangers, and that the individual is powerless against the system. The point is not that this is the message the system is intended to convey, or that the people who work it are not good, kind and helpful. It is the method of organizing human affairs by rational and efficient means, a method inevitable in a complex society, which generates a particular kind of consciousness. This is characterized by feelings of anonymity, by a split between public and private life, and by what Berger and his colleagues refer to as 'the homeless mind'. Berger goes on to draw a religious lesson:

> The 'homelessness' of modern social life has found its most devastating expression in the area of religion. The general uncertainty, both cognitive and normative, brought about by the

25   Peter L. Berger *The Social Reality of Religion*; with B. Berger and H. Kellner, *The Homeless Mind* (1973).

pluralization of everyday life and of biography in modern society, has brought religion into a serious crisis of plausibility. The age-old function of religion – to provide ultimate certainty amid the exigencies of the human condition – has been severely shaken. Because of the religious crisis in modern society, social 'home-lessness' has become metaphysical – that is, it has become 'home-lessness' in the cosmos . . .

Modernity has accomplished many far-reaching transforma-tions, but it has not fundamentally changed the finitude, fragility and mortality of the human condition. What it has done is to seriously weaken those definitions of reality that previously made that condition easier to bear.[26]

The response to this has been to place still further emphasis on private personal forms of religion as individual assertions of identity in face of a world which has become too complex and fragmented.

Whether Berger's account of the function of religion is adequate remains to be discussed. He is often criticized for high-flown gener-alization but, details apart, the kind of relationship he spells out between industrialization, with urbanization as one of its concom-itants, bureaucracy, and the deep-rooted changes in consciousness described earlier, seems to be fairly widely accepted. It does not contain much comfort for my friends in the Middle East, though it could well be asked how far the religious changes observed depend directly on the social changes, or are related to them in some other way. In a subject as complex as this, and as difficult to define with any precision, there is always scope for additional factors to upset the calculations.

Berger does in fact make some interesting comments about the effect of importing bureaucratic structures into Third-World coun-tries, and describes how some aspects of modernity can be accepted without any corresponding significant modernization of conscious-ness. The results are not encouraging, though, in that the form of an industrial society and the form of bureaucracy, without their internal disciplines and constraints, can simply become a recipe for illusion. Berger's comment that 'large numbers of people continue to expect wonders from the State without in the least understanding

26   ibid. (1973), pp. 165–6.

the mechanisms that would be necessary to bring these wonders about,'[27] has applications in so-called modern societies as well.

The struggle to find ways of using the benefits of science without corrupting or disrupting established cultures was a major theme of the World Council of Churches Conference on Faith, Science and the Future in 1979.[28] As a participant at the conference my most abiding impression is of the vehemence of the love/hate relationship towards Western science expressed by representatives from the Third World. Science and technology with all their trappings were seen as the only means of lifting under-developed countries out of their present poverty. Yet the very poverty of such countries lessened their chances of finding alternative patterns of coping with the consequences, by forcing them to compete on terms dictated by those who had already modernized. Nationalism gains attractiveness as one of the ways of resisting the encroachment of an alien culture, and this may be one of the factors in the strong link between religion and national aspirations in the Middle East.

Structural differentiation and secularization of the mind, though they have been described separately, are of course intimately related to one another. Changes in the social significance of religion and its role in society, change personal perceptions of it, and vice versa. A secular society is one in which organized religion is treated as being of only marginal significance, a private pastime for those who like that sort of thing. A secularized mind recognizes religion, if at all, only on the margins of experience. Both factors in the secularizing process push believers and religious institutions in the direction of pluralism and privatization, the themes of the next two chapters.

Before turning to them, however, it is important to note a very different set of reactions to the process of secularization. It has often been pointed out that, so far from being an anti-Christian movement, the secularizing tendencies of the modern world are a logical outcome of the Christian faith. The Old Testament disenchants and moralizes the ancient religion of powers and spirits. The Incarnation roots the sphere of religious activity firmly in this world. The Reformation entailed a further step in the same direction by stripping down faith to the personal response of the individual believer. Barth and Bonhoeffer in their different ways completed the process, Barth

27   ibid., p. 117.
28   W.C.C., *Faith and Science in an Unjust World* (1980).

27

with his claim that Christianity is not a religion capable of being classified as part of some general religious phenomenon, and Bonhoeffer with his tentative and tantalizing explorations of 'religionless Christianity'. Even such an unlikely figure as Thomas Aquinas can be enlisted as an ally, in that one effect of his use of Aristotle was to make possible the laicization of thought. To pinpoint the distinction between a citizen and a faithful Christian is already to have taken a step along the road towards structural differentiation.[29]

It is one thing, however, to see the seeds of secularization in the Christian faith, and another to accept that the way it has actually developed is to be welcomed. Harvey Cox's celebration of the anonymity and freedom of urban life is a good deal less attractive now than when it first appeared in the optimistic 1960s.[30] The same could be said of Munby's *The Idea of a Secular Society*,[31] which tried to encourage Christians to accept the positive values of an open, heterogeneous, tolerant society, held together without any unifying aims and values. Whether such a society can in the long run be stable is more of an open question twenty years later, than it seemed at the time when he wrote.

Berger points to the ironic character of historical relationships.[32] The fact that something grows from Christian seeds does not make it Christian. There are good grounds for claiming that the natural sciences could only have developed in a Christian civilization, but this did not prevent the split in Western consciousness, occasioned by their growth, which is now one of the more disturbing symptoms of secularization. Just as science can bring enormous benefits if it is not allowed to destroy other human values, so the secular society, such as it is, entails enormous gains as well as losses. For the churches to make an adequate response within such a society entails neither pretending that things are now as they always have been in the past, nor relinquishing roles just because they are currently unfashionable. The first requirement is to try to come to a deeper understanding of our society, and of the forces operating within it.

29   Cowling, *Religion and Public Doctrine in Modern England*, pp. 408–10.
30   Harvey Cox, *The Secular City* (1965).
31   D. L. Munby, *The Idea of a Secular Society and Its Significance for Christians* (1963).
32   Berger, *The Social Reality of Religion*, p. 107.

2

Pluralism and Consensus

Descriptions of Britain as a pluralistic society frequently concentrate on the issue of racial pluralism. It was in this sense that I used the term in a diocesan newsletter, written in September 1980, which aroused some interest in the national press at the time, and which I intend to quote at length as setting out the broad issues which form the theme of this chapter.

The key question concerns the future of Britain as a racially mixed community. The word 'pluralist' is used to describe the kind of society in which a variety of different groups, with different beliefs, values and cultures, exist side by side within a larger whole. Many Christians see the growth of pluralism as a God-given means of enlarging human horizons and pressing on to that greater unity of all mankind which is the goal of the Biblical vision of God as 'all in all'. Others see it primarily as an evangelistic opportunity, a mission field on our own door-step. Others are less enthusiastic, and fear a loss of national Christian identity. And there are extreme groups, as we all know, both in this country and elsewhere, which play on this fear and use it to back their demand for racial segregation.

Simple statements about Britain accepting pluralism need rather careful scrutiny, therefore, if we are to understand precisely what is being said, and what we ought to aim for.

In a sense, Britain has always been a pluralist society. We are a hotch-potch of different peoples and cultures which have met and mixed throughout our history, from the Romans to the Vikings, and from the Normans to refugees from Hitler's Germany. In our imperial days we were conscious of belonging to a larger world community on which we had set a British stamp, and there was no hesitation then in stressing the enrichment, both material and cultural, which this brought. Now that we are experiencing colonialism in reverse, as it were, there are temptations to forget our variegated past and the obligations which old ties with other nations still to some extent lay on us.

At each stage in this long process, though, there has been a persistent sense of national identity, and a central core of beliefs, values and customs into which the new influences have mostly been assimilated. The idea that a nation can only be strong and stable if it is united by a single religion and a single culture, was one of the causes of the religious intolerance at the time of the Reformation; much has happened since those days to weaken it, and to demonstrate that people with deep differences between them can in fact live happily together. The growth of tolerance, however, and the consequent development of a more and more pluralist society, has always depended on a residual sense that there are some things which still hold us together as a nation, despite our differences. The greater the diversity, the stronger these residual unifying factors need to be, if the nation is not to become dangerously fragmented. I am not myself convinced that there is single free nation in the world, which has managed to hold a pluralist society together without some very powerful unifying factor.

In Britain we used to have a whole network of such factors, mostly linked in some way to the Church and the Crown. One of the effects of the decline in the national role of the Church has been to isolate the Crown as almost the only effective symbol of national unity. This is one reason why it is desperately important for racial minorities to feel that on the whole 'the powers that be', as symbolized by the Crown, are on their side.

At the same time, I hope the unifying role of the Church – or better still, of all the Christian churches acting together – will not be dismissed too lightly. Attempts to express a Christian viewpoint on some general issue nowadays often meet with the retort that Christian church-goers are only a tiny minority, alongside other minority groups in the nation. Maybe. Nevertheless the emotional and cultural investment by the nation in Christian values and customs remains enormous, and to dismiss this as being of no account, in my view, dangerously underestimates the extent to which our unity as a nation still depends on it.

I am sure we have to take pluralism very seriously. I am

equally convinced that we have to develop and strengthen the things which unite us, and not surrender to the fashionable belief that a nation as such needs no values apart from tolerance.

Clifford Longley, in an article in *The Times*, made a perceptive comment:

Although he separates the Church from the Crown, the Crown also stands for that inheritance. The bishop's argument therefore indirectly and subtly contradicts the claim that the British monarchy should have no relationship to morality or religion in a pluralistic society. His argument also elevates the issue of disestablishment of the Church of England to the highest plane, for if there was no national church there would be no place for Christianity, and no public constitutional symbol indicating that certain beliefs and values were particularly more British than any other.[1]

But is the argument of my letter sound? Peter Hinchliff, in an interesting exploration of the same theme, admits that it has some force: 'It may be true that in Britain Christianity is the only religion which could possibly make a bid to act as the symbol of national tolerance.'[2] Nevertheless he doubts whether any attempt to restore the 'throne and altar' view of society can be convincing in a country which now contains so many people of other faiths.

There are, however, more general reasons for doubting the validity of the argument, reasons which would operate just as powerfully even if there had been no substantial immigration into Britain in the post-war years. Modern societies, it is claimed, are pluralist by nature. Racial pluralism is a symptom of this, and may sharpen the conflicts. But the idea that any one religious group can act as a basis for social cohesion in a society as fragmented as modern Britain, even without the complications of non-Christian faiths, is regarded as highly dubious.

My aim in this chapter is to scrutinize such doubts, first by considering the notion of pluralism itself, then by trying to evaluate the role of the wide variety of substructures in a modern society, and their relation to the State, and finally by attempting to estimate the extent to which this complex interaction of agencies and forces

1   *The Times*, 22 September 1980.
2   Peter Hinchliff, *Holiness and Politics* (1982), p. 27.

still depends for its health and effectiveness on a residuum of shared values.

Berger is a forceful exponent of the view that there is an intimate causal relationship between pluralism and secularization.[3] According to him the main characteristic of modern life is that it is rationalized and segmented. In a differentiated society the public frame of religious symbolism loses its hold, and individuals are driven more and more to treat religion as purely a matter of private choice. Urbanization, modern means of communication, modern educational policies, mobility and rootlessness, all contribute to the process. Individuals are bombarded with a multiplicity of experiences, information and opinion. In place of religious or social consensus, there is a supermarket of faiths and ideals, in which different heritages are packaged to suit the preferences of individual consumers. The net result is that no one tradition can any longer represent the values and aspirations of a whole nation, if it ever could. The effect on individuals, insofar as they keep themselves open to the variety of opinion (and 'openness' has become a modern value) is to create permanent crises of identity.

How much is cause and how much is effect in this highly compressed account of modern pluralism is doubtless a matter for argument. Berger may well be dubbed more of a social historian than a social theorist.[4] Martin questions whether British society is as pluralist nowadays as it was in the heyday of religious dissent.[5] But that pluralism runs very deep in modern societies is not, I believe, seriously open to question. Nor must it be seen as requiring the existence of coherent and well-organized alternatives to a dominant Christian tradition. There can be a pluralism of doubt as well as a pluralism of faiths, a variety of ways of not being Christian, which do not imply positive commitment to belief in something else.[6]

Such a society has evident strengths as well as possible weaknesses. Britain does not seem to be suffering from the crisis of 'ungovernability' which was predicted a few years ago. Despite social strains and serious inequalities, the 1977 Gallup-poll finding that the British people are among the happiest in the world is still

3   Berger, *The Social Reality of Religion*, p. 134, etc.
    Berger, Berger and Kellner, *The Homeless Mind*, p. 63, 76 etc.
4   Glasner, *The Sociology of Secularization*, p. 55.
5   David Martin, *The Dilemmas of Contemporary Religion* (1978), p. 12.
6   Gilbert, *The Making of Post-Christian Britain*, pp. 36–8.

probably near the truth.[7] In my 1980 letter I referred to the positive welcome given to a pluralist, multi-cultural society by Christians working in the field of race relations, and the British Council of Churches, as might be expected, has been a consistent advocate of this broad-based, open-handed approach to social diversity. Beyond these particular concerns, however, there lies a much larger and more fundamental issue, the claim that a pluralistic society is essential for the promotion and safeguarding of individual freedom.

This was the issue which dominated discussions about pluralism in Britain at the turn of the century. For Neville Figgis[8] and his colleagues the secular tolerant state, with no overall aims and ideology of its own, but simply holding the ring for the multiplicity of groups of which it is composed, as a 'society of societies', was the best guarantee of liberty. Given that liberty itself is the overriding value, then a minimal view of the State, with power dispersed rather than concentrated, follows as an inevitable consequence. Any attempt to impose an artificial unity on people whose values and interests do in fact differ can only arouse fear and resentment among minority groups; and the end of that road, it was said, is likely to be totalitarianism or civil war.

We shall return to Figgis a little later. Meanwhile we need to note the other side of the picture, the fears of instability which too uncritical an acceptance of pluralism can generate.

On a very simple estimate of social order, stability might be thought to depend on the existence of at least some shared values. For most of the time it may be possible for people to work together on the basis of a tacit consensus, or even on the basis of a supposed consensus which hides the disagreements.[9] The mass media, for example, may give the impression of a greater degree of unity than actually exists. But there are occasions in the life of any group when the degree of consensus is tested, and it is then that there has to be an appeal beyond the particular interests represented to some higher legitimating value or authority. But where does this reside? In a secular pluralist society shared values and recognized authorities are the fruits of consensus, not the basis of it. If there is no higher authority than the State itself, and if there are real and deep divisions which lead to a breakdown in the consensus, what then is to

7 Arthur Marwick, *British Society since 1945* (1982), pp. 227, 271.
8 D. Nicholls, *The Pluralist State* (1975), *passim.*
9 Kelvin, *The Bases of Social Behaviour*, pp. 27, 31.

be done? Values and authorities which are merely the fruits of consensus lose their power just when they are most needed. The appeal to tradition, as a kind of 'consensus in time', might have a certain stabilizing effect. But logically the conclusion seems inescapable that a fully pluralist state, which was that and nothing more, could only survive by drawing from time to time on values outside its own commitment to pluralism.

Norman is sceptical not only about the stability of such a society, but about its existence. On his view a so-called 'pluralistic' society is inherently unstable because it is a society 'in transition from one set of orthodoxies to another'.[10] Like much of what he deplores in present-day social analysis, 'talk about the values of a "pluralistic" society ignores a lot of hidden class reference. Most of the components of the plurality, when examined, turn out to exist only within the professional class and intelligentsia – there is much greater agreement about the moral bases of society within the working-classes.'

There may well be truth in this, but Norman seems a little too ready to use differing class perceptions as an all-purpose excuse for dismissing uncomfortable evidence. Some of the evidence at least suggests that the working-classes are just as much influenced by pluralism as the intelligentsia; after all, it is they who generally live next door to immigrants. The working-classes, too, are at the sharp end of many of the contradictions in our present society, and there is evidence that in terms of the images by which they have to live, they share its confusions.[11] The claim that pluralistic societies are inherently transitional has more to commend it, and I suspect that what Norman ought to have said is that while all experience the advantages and disadvantages of living in a pluralistic society, intellectuals and those influenced by them are more ready to go on living with the idea of it, and more likely to give a positive value to its ambiguities and instabilities.

Advocates of pluralism do not deny its potential instability. They simply point to the fact that there is no generally accepted value system, certainly not one based on religion, capable of holding a modern society together. The churches are too weak and the cults

10   Norman, *Church and Society in England*, p. 427.
11   Martin Bulmer (ed.), *Working-Class Images of Society* (1975), p. 155.

are too ephemeral.[12] There are, however, techniques and structures which maintain stability, and to these we must now turn.

I recall a revealing conversation in Beirut with the Director of Al Makassed, a large private educational foundation for Muslims in the Middle East. In describing the characteristics of Muslim society he pointed to its comparative lack of social institutions in contrast with Western society. Muslims have few intermediate organizations or voluntary bodies filling the social gap between the family and the State. The result is a certain deficiency in social finesse and, although he did not say it in so many words, a danger of drifting either towards indifference concerning the State, or towards extremism. A rich social sub-structure was envied as a source of resilience.

This perception, coming from a totally different culture, matches exactly the importance ascribed by Figgis, as well as by contemporary commentators, to the variety of institutional life in a modern society.[13] Thousands of organizations, from interest groups like local angling clubs to pressure groups like the political parties, from churches to photographic associations and from football supporters' clubs to Christian Aid, enrich the texture of society – and provide opportunities for people to meet, to find significance, to create linkages and to express their personal values. Some, like trade unions, exist primarily for the benefit of their members. Others, like charitable organizations, have their *raison d'etre* in the service of others, though there may well be personal satisfactions in belonging to them. Insofar as the different groups and organizations interweave and overlap, they help to strengthen social bonds, and ideally, according to Figgis, the State should be no more than a neutral context within which they can interact, and a preserver of their liberties.

The churches were in some sense the pioneers of this variety. In Figgis's words, 'Political liberty is the fruit of ecclesiastical animosity.'[14] It is not, as frequently claimed, that political toleration grew out of exhaustion following the post-Reformation religious struggle, but that minority churches struggled, in the end successfully, for

12 R. H. Preston, 'Secularization and Renewal' in *Crucible* (1977), pp. 68–76.

13 A. H. Hanson and Malcolm Walles, *Governing Britain* (1980 edn), ch. 7.

14 Quoted in Nicholls, p. 33.

35

freedom of speech and freedom of association. Tolerant pluralism was born out of this success, with the recognition that there was no way in which competing religious groups could subdue one another. Far from threatening the stability of the State, this break-up of the religious consensus actually strengthened it by creating different religious frameworks capable of legitimating different political stances. Conflict could thus be accepted and absorbed and still held within an overall Christian context.

Our own experience of pluralism, seventy years after Figgis wrote, is much more complex, not only because of the more complex religious situation, but because his idea of the tolerant liberal State has proved plainly inadequate. The idea that a rich institutional life in some way prepares people for citizenship and aids social cohesion, remains a powerful one, though. Durkheim claimed that a State disintegrates without 'a series of secondary groups near enough to individuals to attract them . . . and drag them into the general torrent of social life'.[15]

Kingman Brewster, a former U.S. Ambassador to Britain, has described how for many people the greatest purpose and satisfaction in life is to be found in the 'self-determined sector'.[16] Local voluntary organizations, small enough to enable those who belong to them to see the difference they are making, provide the main life-chance for people who feel more and more dominated by the bigness and impersonality of the modern world. They encourage what Brewster calls a 'selfish usefulness', a desire to be known and wanted and to make one's contribution, not in a moralistic way but in a way which draws out the potential of those involved. Such groups are the cement of society.

The churches are obviously capable of fulfilling this kind of role, especially if they avoid a sectarian preoccupation with their own members. But not all organizations and groups have this beneficial effect. Groups may tyrannize over one another, and over their members. They can reproduce on a smaller scale some of the ills of the society in which they are set; the growth of bureaucracy in the churches is a case in point. They can also pursue their own interests in ways which are damaging to those who are not so well organized. The operation of pressure groups, long recognized as an essential

15   ibid., p. 55.
16   Kingman Brewster, 'Purpose in a Voluntary Society' in *The Cambridge Review*, vol. 103 (1982), p. 327.

feature of United States democracy, can be conducted in more than one style. Nicholls comments how, rather than devoting their energies to their main ends, thus minimizing the need for Government interference, they compete with one another to influence Government policy, thus maximizing the role of the State.[17] This is a far cry from Figgis's ideal of voluntary organizations as the mainspring of social action, with the Government simply acting as a referee.

The choice between these alternatives has clear contemporary political implications in Britain. There are other questions, too, which need to be asked about this particular vision of the pluralist state. Is liberty the only value to be preserved? And if other ideals, equality for instance, are pursued at national level, is this compatible with the neutrality towards fundamental values, which a strict pluralism might seem to entail?

For the moment, however, the main point of the argument concerns the significance for a nation of a rich institutional life. It seems clear that, when due allowance is made for the fact that not all groups and organizations contribute to social stability, on the whole a complex society, representing many shifting and competing interests, is more stable than a simple one.[18] To repeat a word used earlier, it is more resilient. A monolithic society, dominated by a particular group or a particular set of ideas, may look more stable, but may in fact be subverted more easily. Monolithic societies either tend to crack, or to be taken over in their entirety by dictators. To this extent the worry expressed by T. S. Eliot in his *The Idea of a Christian Society*, about the lack of Christian consensus in modern societies, begins to look unreal.[19] Certainly from the point of view of the nation there may be positive advantages in not having too tight a consensus, though how far the complete disavowal of shared values can safely be taken has already been questioned, and needs to be considered further.

From the point of view of the individual Christian, though, as for any member of a minority group, pluralism has its dangers. In striking contrast with Kierkegaard, whose problem was exactly the opposite, Eliot spelt out the difficulty of being Christian in a non-believing society.

17 Nicholls, p. 118.
18 S. Budd, *Sociologists and Religion* (1973), p. 72; see also Martin, *A General Theory of Secularization, passim.*
19 T. S. Eliot, *The Idea of a Christian Society* (1939).

Like every minority we compound with necessity, learning to speak the language of the dominant culture because those whose language it is will not speak ours; in speaking their language we are always in danger of thinking their thoughts and behaving according to their code.[20]

This fear of cultural pollution is one of the destabilizing factors in the kind of pluralist society so far described. The rich network of competing interests can work satisfactorily in matters where not too much is at stake. But in matters where genial tolerance is not felt to be adequate, the groups and organizations tend to be driven further and further away from one another, and into a kind of sectarian isolation. This is true politically as well as religiously, and may be one of the reasons for the fissiparous tendencies of the political left.

A pluralist society may thus make it more difficult for people to care deeply about anything, while still remaining in the mainstream of social life. This has never been easy, as the monastic movement illustrates, but at least the monks were recognized for what they were by the society around them, whereas nowadays excessive zeal is likely to cause social embarrassment. The exception is when some major crisis restores a sense of national unity, and this perhaps explains the slightly shamefaced excitement felt during the Falklands war. It is interesting, too, that part of the political response to the war was to heighten the significance of the main social legitimating agencies, however residual their function in more normal circumstances. Thus the Church of England found itself thrust into the limelight.

Small incidents like these, as well as more general worries like Eliot's, suggest that there are, or ought to be, limits to pluralism. There are other problems too. Although it is possible to visualize in broad terms how a complex network of structures within the body of a State may make it both more stable and more flexible, it is harder to be certain in practice just how effectively this works. It is also by no means certain that this kind of structure can supply all that is needed to replace a more traditional concern with national aims and values.

Take the case of the Labour Party. In a lengthy discussion of what he calls 'fraternity', Halsey refers to the constant problem

20 Quoted in Cowling, *Religion and Public Doctrine*, p. 127.

encountered by the labour movement in transforming local loyalties into national ones.[21] Working-class strength lies in the close social networks around the work place or the street. Highly fraternal organizations, Friendly Societies, Co-ops, Miners' Lodges, and such like were the birthplace of the party, and the national organization grew from the bottom upwards. In doing so it inevitably changed its character. It became a bureaucracy like any other bureaucracy, with all that that entails in terms of 'them' and 'us'. Ironically the principle of mutual voluntary help which had sustained the local organizations, was discounted at national level by opposition to the principle of philanthropy; statutory rights had to replace charitable endeavour. Ideals and experiences, in other words, are not easily transferable when there is a change of scale. Insofar as this is perceived by those involved, the resulting disillusionment creates favourable conditions for a rise of direct action groups, which try to avoid the fate of the main party by subversion of the political process.

It is possible to see the same process in reverse in a traditional Labour-held borough in my own diocese. A long-standing paternalistic regime, concerned to offer the highest standards of social care, has had the effect of depressing, and even actively discouraging, the growth of local voluntary organizations. This has dried up the pool of concerned citizens with some knowledge of public life, which in turn has eroded the quality of the elected representatives. Both statutory and voluntary organizations have thus gone into decline together.

Although I have referred specifically to the Labour Party, the problems are general ones. The quality of national life depends on the quality of local life, and vice versa, but the links between them are subtle, and there is no direct route from one to the other.

The point is well made by Peter Laslett in an essay on the face-to-face society,[22] in which he describes the difficulties encountered in scaling up the pattern of classical Athenian democracy to a larger national society. The ideal of active personal participation by people relating to one another as whole people, breaks down as soon as it is applied to anything larger than a small city-state. Aristotle was aware of the problem and described it as a task 'for divine power'.

21 A. H. Halsey, *Change in British Society* (1981 edn), pp. 57, 85.
22 Peter Laslett (ed.), *Philosophy, Politics and Society* (1970), pp. 177–83.

Laslett elaborates the phrase by drawing a parallel between religious psychology and the shift in political perspective required. Individual vision has to be expanded through a system of representation. There has to be a sense of community with the unseen, and identification with some supreme authority or source of sovereignty, a use of symbolism which enables the larger society to be represented in its wholeness. He even instances a kind of appeal to 'revelation', in the shape of a nation's history and tradition.

This is not an invitation to pass too swiftly and easily from the problem of national identity to the claim that it needs religious validation. The point is rather that the question, what is it that enables a nation to hold together and function as a nation? has many dimensions to it, some of which are religious in character.

Answers so far given to it in this chapter have been in general terms, and have concentrated on the importance of a rich and complex sub-structure of institutions, of which the churches themselves are examples. We must now look in more detail at some of the other factors, in particular political ones, which are said to hold Britain together as a nation, and ask whether they too have a hidden religious dimension.

The simplest and most straightforward answer to the question of British national unity is that the nation is held together by agreement on certain procedures. Deep political and other differences can be contained, if there is agreement about the framework within which conflicts are allowed to take place. And that framework is parliamentary. Political consensus is often spoken of as if it referred primarily to the broad similarities between the policies of the main parties. At any one time such a consensus may or may not exist. But what must exist, if the political process is not to break down completely, is a general consensus about the way the process ought to work.

The fundamental questions about social cohesion, on this view, are constitutional, not political, and it is on this constitutional level that we must first examine the sources of stability.[23] And it is here, of course, that Britain's peculiarity is most evident.

Dependency on the sovereignty of the Queen in Parliament, in the absence of any written constitution, has given British political

23 For this whole section I rely heavily on Nevil Johnson, *In Search of the Constitution: Reflections on State and Society in Britain* (1976), especially chapters 3 and 8.

life a flexibility which is highly valued by those involved in it. The unlimited sovereignty of Parliament is not in practice as great as it might seem in theory, since there are laws which relate to constitutional matters even if they do not add up to anything approaching a constitution. The main emphasis, however, is on a network of conventions, assumptions and unwritten understandings, which are justified on the ground that they enable Parliament to respond to political reality in ways impossible to nations more tightly bound by written rules.

In the days when the force of convention was strong, and ideas of authority and tradition were generally respected, the system undoubtedly worked well. Today, however, there are those who wonder whether it is adequate to our changed political circumstances, and in particular whether it provides sufficient safeguards against 'the relentless extension of public power'. Flexibility is fine, and the sovereignty of Parliament is fine, as long as the conventional restraints and the common understandings have firm enough roots to withstand rough handling. But have they? And what is it that nourishes them? The threat is not just to parliamentary conventions which, in the light of the clubability of both Houses of Parliament, are probably safer than most. It touches more these wider conventions, and the nourishment of the more personal qualities, on which public life is based.

Reference to the constitution as a basis for stability thus leads very quickly to a search for ways in which the conventions which support it are embodied in national and political life.

The Common Law tradition is one such embodiment, as is current concern about Human Rights. Both have helped to feed the notion of 'citizenship', which is now regarded by some as one of the most useful categories of political self-understanding.[24] Insofar as ordinary citizens are aware of their complex pattern of industrial, social and political rights, and are encouraged to value their common experience of citizenship as part of more or less egalitarian society, the roots of political life are nourished, and individuals have something to throw into the balance against the encroachments of centralized power.[25]

But does this describe what actually happens in modern Britain?

24 D. Lockwood in *Sociology*, vol. 8 (1974), p. 365.
25 Halsey, p. 162.

There are good reasons to fear that the emphasis on rights, so far from strengthening social cohesion, has in fact reduced it by seeming to justify an individualistic kind of acquisitiveness. Furthermore, talk about 'a more or less egalitarian society' in a time of high unemployment, fails to reckon with the deep legacy of social division which such unemployment is bound to leave even if, which seems unlikely, some economic method can be found for reducing it. Add to these economic strains the strains of ethnic pluralism, and the ambiguous views on citizenship which emerged in the long debate on the Nationality Bill, and it is clear that the notion of citizenship as a basis for social cohesion is fairly fragile.

A very different kind of embodiment of the conventions supporting national life is to be found in the Civil Service tradition.[26] Here, like the constitution itself, is an object of legitimate pride which has served the nation well. But there are also problems.

At one level the Civil Service acts like any other bureaucracy with its hierarchical structure, its dependence on rules, and the high value placed on tradition and precedent. The system itself has a socializing effect by imposing its own values on those who operate it, both consciously and unconsciously, and its role in promoting secularization has already been mentioned in a previous chapter. There are general problems about the creeping growth of bureaucracy and what this does to the character of a society, but these are not my prime concern at the moment. The point of interest is the point where this largely self-sustaining system brings its values and conventions to bear on the political life of the nation.

In practical terms the doubts, now being expressed by a number of commentators, concern the relationship between top civil servants and their Ministers; in particular whether the high integrity and degree of commitment required of such civil servants can go on being combined in all circumstances with total political neutrality. The distinction between expert advisers and actual decision-makers is, of course, fundamental to political life in this country.[27] The problem is that it presupposes a distinction between facts and values which cannot in practice be sustained. It also presupposes that even in matters of the most profound importance, people of integrity can, as it were, 'switch values' at command.

26 Johnson, ch. 6.
27 Hanson and Walles (p. 160), who take the opposite point of view from Johnson.

In reality, perhaps, things may be very different, and it may well be that the kind of relationships described in the TV programme 'Yes Minister', as well as in some ministerial diaries, are nearer to the truth than the idealized picture generally painted. But to acknowledge this only sharpens the problem. The values expressed, whether overtly or indirectly, and the conventions observed by those who stand at the centre of public life, have in the end to be related to personal values, if the whole exericse is not to suffer from an inner corruption. The source of these values is thus a matter of some interest.

In part, as already suggested, they derive from within the system itself. All professions socialize their own members, and values which may originally have been deliberately imported, as from the classical Greats tradition at Oxford (one of the main nurseries of top-level civil servants) become more or less self-sustaining. But this can never be the whole story. Or if it is, it becomes a recipe for sterility and stagnation. The need for some fresh input is illustrated by the reliance of central government on the services of those described as 'the Great and the Good'. The kind of people who are called upon for advice in controversial matters, or who help to restore the integrity of public life when things go wrong, are usually people who have themselves been nourished by some source of excellence outside the political system.

The point being made is an obvious one, namely that procedures and conventions and hallowed institutions may not by themselves be enough to ensure the inner integrity and stability of national life. It has been felt necessary to make it at some length, if only because some writers seem to assume that they are.

Mention was made earlier of the importance of symbols as a means of harnessing loyalties and energies, generated elsewhere, in the service of wider national concerns. Attachment to symbols operates on a different level and among a much larger constituency than the rather elitist respect for conventions discussed in the last few paragraphs. A nation needs more than integrity at the top; it needs some focal point of affectionate identification which operates powerfully among those at the bottom as well.

There is no need to elaborate on the significance of the Monarchy as a symbol of national unity, all the more effective for being personal. It is an open question whether a constitution as loose and flexible as the British one could survive without this strong symbolic

43

element at its centre. Its religious connotations have been drawn out in the quotation from Clifford Longley earlier in this chapter.

Of more immediate concern is the question whether the idea of national identity itself can be an aid to social cohesion. The problems about it are posed in their sharpest form by Enoch Powell. His so-called racism has its origins in a typically logical exercise in analysis. According to him,

> the nation is the one social unit which, on the secular plane at least, provides a satisfying frame of reference for men's individual hopes and ambitions; and . . . the only nation I can recognize as my own is that defined by allegiance to the Crown in Parliament . . .[28]

He then goes on to state his belief 'that self-identification of each part with the whole is the one essential precondition of being a parliamentary nation'. The argument concludes that while some individuals coming from different cultures may achieve this self-identification, immigrant communities numbered in millions will not. Therefore, in the interests of national identity, they must go. The same argument is used to oppose British membership of the European Community. National sovereignty is all.

Logic, however, cannot undo the facts, the most important of which are that Britain is in some measure a pluralist society already, and that strong assertions of national identity are increasingly unreal in a world where policies have to be dictated more and more by international, rather than national, considerations. Sovereignty can no longer be all, because the world no longer works that way. Nor can the ideal of 'the self-identification of each part with the whole' be a condition of nationhood, because one of the problems of modern highly differentiated societies is precisely how to achieve that self-identification. The presence of separate ethnic communities adds a new dimension to the problem, but does not create it. Thus in following through the logic of the idea of national identity, Powell only succeeds in exposing its weakness.

It is true that in some circumstances assertions of national identity can be a powerful unifying force.[29] This is particularly so in periods of national growth, or in the face of external threats. But in

28 Enoch Powell, *Wrestling with the Angel* (1977), pp. 4–5.
29 Berger, Berger and Kellner, p. 149.

the circumstances of Britain today, uncertainty about national identity, and the search for some firm basis of social cohesion, are all part of the same problem. The Monarchy stands outside this self-questioning, which is why it is still symbolically effective.

Another way of trying to identify the basis of social cohesion is in terms which make a more explicit reference to values, especially traditional ones. A society can live for a long time on a store of accumulated wisdom. This is especially true in a country which thrives on nostalgia, and whose people have a kind of native caution, a respect for tradition and a suspicion of large abstract proposals for change. This has both political and religious dimensions. Conservative Christian thinkers justify resistance to change in terms of the doctrine of original sin; human interference, based on human imperfection, on the whole only makes bad things worse. Quinton[30] claims that a secular version of the same doctrine has always undergirded Conservative political thinking, and Marwick[31] has coined the phrase 'secular Anglicanism' as a description of the same sort of phenomenon in society at large. Secular Anglicanism shows tolerance and resilience verging on complacency; it is the expression of British adaptability and pragmatism. Though under threat from some of the growing divisions in British society, it succeeded in carrying the country through the disruptions of the 1960s and the more recent 'winters of discontent' without fatal damage to the fundamentally humane tradition of public life.

But what nourishes its roots? Is it just a manifestation of British character, whatever that might mean? Or is it, as its name suggests, a hang-over from non-secular Anglicanism? And is it in any case the kind of tradition likely to go on appealing to those who find it increasingly hard to feel they have a real stake in the life of the nation? – or in a society where performance consistently fails to match up to expectations? Subtle, flexible, balanced traditions can survive a great many changes, but they are under special strain when the relationship between the generations is weak, when young people grow up with little sense of history and little to look forward to, and when claims to authority are apt to be regarded with suspicion.

The nourishment of such attitudes and traditions is especially

30 Anthony Quinton, *The Politics of Imperfection* (1978).
31 Marwick, pp. 16, 154, 277, etc.

important in Britain in view of our constitutional dependence on unwritten rules. But there is a wider sense in which the quality of government in any country, however comprehensive its constitution, depends on the moral and political maturity of its people. And that in turn depends on having aims and values beyond politics. Dorothy Emmet refers to 'a good beyond politics which politicians can acknowledge, and thereby bring their own task into perspective'.[32] Finally in this chapter, therefore, we must consider what some of these values might be.

In a famous essay on 'Politics as a Vocation'[33] Max Weber pinpointed the three pre-eminent qualities for a politician as 'passion, a feeling of responsibility, and a sense of proportion'. Passion entails a vision of some great good to be sought; responsibility entails a proper relationship with those whom the politician represents, as well as with the hard realities of the situation in which he finds himself; proportion implies distance, a proper relationship with himself and his own ambitions.

It would not be hard to add to the list. Disinterestedness, tolerance, generosity, faith, perseverance might all possibly be seen as variants or fruits of Weber's primary qualities; others might wish to add harsher qualities like ruthlessness,[34] or more flamboyant ones which he described elsewhere as 'charisma'. Whatever the precise content of the list, the fact that some special qualities are needed poses the question of how they are to be nurtured. For a mature political process to work, there need to be at least some people of moral stature in each generation, who share at least some of the qualities required. Not all such people, by any means, are nurtured in a religious tradition, but Weber's list has enough religious overtones to make one pause and ask whether the religious contribution at this stage in the political process can be written off as easily as some of its critics suppose.

Beyond the particular qualities required of those who are active politicians, there is a broader spread of less demanding qualities required of the populace at large. Marwick's 'secular Anglicanism' describes some of them. Phrases like 'good neighbourliness', 'working together', 'faith in the future', 'caring and sharing', say some-

32 Dorothy Emmet, *The Moral Prism* (1979), p. 30.
33 Max Weber, *Essays in Sociology*, (O.U.P., 1958 edn), p. 115.
34 T. Nagel, 'Ruthlessness in Public Life' in S. Hampshire (ed.), *Public and Private Morality* (1978).

thing at a simple practical level about qualities which are felt to go into the making of a good society. The things which make people feel they belong to one another, and share some responsibility for one another, no doubt have deep roots in the process whereby all of us grow up as social beings but, as at the more sophisticated level, the religious overtones cannot be ignored.

The quality of disinterestedness poses particular problems for those who see its social importance, and want to detach it from religious roots. Wilson puts this as one of the main question-marks over the ability of a purely secular society to maintain itself without religion.

> The disinterested devotion which was vital to the creation of the capitalist work order and to the public life of industrial nations, and which rested on a religious idea-system, appears as a type of moral capital debt which is no longer being serviced.[35]

Attempts have been made in some circles to discover a natural, biological basis for altruism. A new branch of science, socio-biology, has as its central feature an ingenious theory demonstrating the evolutionary advantage of sacrificing oneself for one's kin. It is not without its difficulties, but the subject is too large to enter into now.[36] Even if the theory does what it claims, however, and it becomes generally accepted that human beings have some natural altruistic impulses, the practical problems of developing and fostering these remain. The most unlikely human beings can rise to marvellous heights, but disinterestedness is not a quality which is very evident in society as a whole.

Faith and hope, likewise, are qualities which depend on a typically religious attitude to life. It is true that they have their secular counterparts, and there are plenty of hopes entertained in the political sphere which have nothing whatever to do with Christian hope. There may be a thin dividing line between hope and illusion. But the ability to hold on to what is unseen, and to work for it despite opposition, discouragement and failure, is the essence of the quality, and the fact that it may be attached to some aim which is

35 B. Wilson, *Religion in Secular Society*, pp. 231–3.
36 E. O. Wilson's *On Human Nature* (1978) is a seminal work. There is a useful philosophical critique in Roger Trigg's *The Shaping of Man* (1982).

unworthy or illusory is, for our present purposes, of secondary importance.

The reference to failure brings us to the quality which is perhaps most neglected in public life, and where Christians may have most to offer. A key difference between Christianity and secular Humanism is that Christians have, or ought to have, more effective ways of dealing with failure.[37] A gospel of forgiveness is utterly different from advice to try harder. Within the political sphere the importance of some way of undoing hurts, dissolving grievances and 'releasing power from its own perversions', can hardly be overstressed.

Haddon Willmer[38] has explored this theme, and made the interesting point that perhaps a pluralist society, more than any other, needs the quality of forgiveness. The alternative is for parties in conflict to go their separate ways.

From a rather different perspective Bruce Reed has proposed a theory of religious activity,[39] which gives a central place to the experiences of weakness, inadequacy, failure and conflict. Everyone, he claims, needs some healthy way of regressing into a relationship of dependence which, if handled properly, can act as a kind of death and resurrection. The main social function of religion, in this theory, is to recharge the springs of action, to turn worshippers around to face life again with renewed hope and energy, and to send them out to do their work in the world with a fresh vision of the kingdom of God. We shall return to Reed's theory in chapter 5. Meanwhile it is simply listed as one of the many examples of how insights about the health of society weave in and out of religious insights.

There is no means of knowing, apart from the perspectives of history, how far Britain, if it becomes more secular and pluralist, will still depend for its stability on its residual religious roots. This chapter began with a question about the validity of an argument, and no more can be given in reply than hints and suggestions. At each point in the survey of the various factors which seem to contribute to social stability in Britain, there have been unanswered questions and indications that by themselves merely secular insti-

37 This once struck me very strongly in a conversation with Marghanita Laski.
38 Hadden Willmer, 'Forgiveness and Politics' in *Crucible* (1979), pp. 100–5.
39 Bruce Reed, *The Dynamics of Religion: Process and Movement in Christian Churches* (1978).

tutions and procedures are not enough. Religious questions keep intruding and religious values are never far from the surface. But whatever the precise relationship between religion and public life in Britain, it is certain that it is both complex and manifold.

In the first place, religious bodies are the largest voluntary agencies in the country, and therefore on any reckoning make a massive contribution to the richness of institutional life, and to the social training and support of individuals.

Secondly, they nurture, both directly and indirectly, many of the values and general attitudes on which the conduct of public life depends, not least in their ability to challenge and disturb, as well as to heal and restore. It is not claimed that the churches are the sole source of such values, only that they are an important source, and that some important values seem to belong particularly within a religious context.

Thirdly, religion meets the need for a public language of hope, aspiration, penitence and renewal even though the particular languages of particular religious bodies are no longer fully accessible to more than a minority.

Fourthly, Britain has maintained a formal public commitment to the Christian faith, expressed in part through the Monarchy, while in practice acknowledging a substantial degree of pluralism. Though on the face of it illogical, symbolic expressions of unity can be important, even when they no longer correspond closely with political realities. The power of symbolism does not depend on its logical tidiness; in fact it may be all the greater for not being reduced to size within a rationalistic framework.

Fifthly, as will be suggested later, there is a specific Christian contribution to be made towards the understanding and attainment of unity. This is linked with the themes of forgiveness and creativity, and goes far beyond the simple assertions about the importance of religious values, which have been one of the main burdens of this chapter.

As will be seen, there is much more to be said. The description of the role of the churches given thus far has been deliberately lop-sided. Christianity is not just about values. Nor is its primary purpose to secure social stability, though this may in practice emerge as one of its useful functions. A faith reduced to this role, however, would have become as secularized as the society in which it is set.

3

Public Life and Private Life

'Privatization' is an ugly word, but unfortunately there is no alternative with quite the same meaning. With 'secularization' and 'pluralism' it forms part of the trilogy of symptoms said to be characteristic of modern societies. To privatize an activity is to relate it more and more exclusively to the private sphere of life. Religion has been privatized in modern societies, it is claimed, as a result of the progressive weakening or disappearance of the public framework of religious belief and apprehension. Religious believers can no longer rely on the unquestioned assumptions of the society in which they live. Belief has become a matter of private choice.

There has, of course, always been a sense in which individuals have had to choose whether, or how far, to commit themselves to a particular religious faith. Evidence was presented in chapter 1 to show how the idea of a primitive religious consciousness in which once upon a time all members of a given society participated uncritically, does not square with the facts. The characteristic of modern societies is not choice as such, but the wide range of available options. Faced with a range of options, choice becomes more a matter of personal predilections. At the extreme, its significance is reduced to that of a mere expression of opinion.

Berger describes how modern man can now shop around for his beliefs in a religious supermarket.[1] The more goods there are on display, the more individual the choice becomes, and the more likely it is to be influenced by attractive packaging rather than by any essential difference between the contents. Churches all acting under the same social pressures tend to conform to the same basic model, but with undue emphasis on the marginal differences which make them appear distinctive. No doubt the analogy applies more

1 Berger, *The Social Reality of Religion*, p. 137.

closely to the American religious scene than to the British, but the connection between pluralism and privatization seems plain enough.

Interestingly supermarkets can themselves be seen as symptoms of privatization. Whether one is shopping for faith or for instant coffee, the style they impose reflects the individual, private, character of the choice. There is an anonymity and an impersonality in being one of a crowd making one's personal selection, in marked contrast to the communal pressures at work in a local corner shop.

Privatization, in fact, is not just a religious phenomenon. The nuclear family, mother, father, and two children, separated from their other relatives, and cut off from their neighbours in their high-rise flat, can exhibit all the classic symptoms. They live segmented lives, with mother and father going their different ways to jobs and the children gaining their experience in huge anonymous schools. They encounter the public world through the private medium of their television set. They shop in a supermarket, and go away for the weekend in a private car. They do not recognizably 'belong' anywhere.

Such a family may find itself under extreme pressures.[2] Its members have to discover and affirm much of their personal significance within a limited set of close relationships. The family, or some close family-like group, may be forced into a role in which it carries the weight of religious or quasi-religious meaning formerly carried by a publicly validated religious framework. This is one reason for the attractiveness of some modern cults, with their strong emphasis on the group itself as a family substitute. The Moonies actually call themselves 'the family', and reinforce their exclusiveness by deliberately breaking their members' bonds with their natural families. The churches, too, particularly in the kind of housing estates where privatization is very marked, consciously exploit their family image. In some cases language about 'the church family' has been used to a degree which puts considerable strain on those whose own experience of family life does not conform to the image.

The general thrust within a privatized society, however, is against most kinds of church or other associational life. The frequent lament that it is 'difficult to get people to come to meetings', or 'to go out at night' is heard right across the social spectrum and over a wide

2   Martin, *A General Theory of Secularization*, p. 89.

range of activities. The privatized worker, for instance, is apt to see his trade union as 'less the symbolic expression of an affective attachment to a working-class community than a utilitarian association for achieving his private goal of a rising standard of living'.[3] Poor attendance at meetings reflects this concern. There is a weakness, in fact, in the social sub-structure described in the last chapter, and privatization is one of the factors which eats away at the social cohesion of a pluralist society, as well as being both a cause and a product of that society.

As the last sentence suggests, the relationship between cause and effect in the development of privatization is highly complex. A major ecclesiastical element has clearly been the growth of denominationalism. Bound up with this have been changes in attitudes towards authority, towards the value of tolerance, towards the exclusiveness and finality of religious truth. Other factors like the segmentation of life in modern societies, and the imposition of a bureaucratic stamp on the character of many relationships, have all been parts of the same story. So has the growth of affluence.[4] On a simple view of things, modern technology and industrialization have provided the means for people to escape from one another. Increased mobility is perhaps the biggest single cause of the break-up of the more settled and community-orientated type of society. And so one might go on. But for our present purpose the distinction between cause and effect is not important. It is the implications of the whole package of causes and effects, with privatization as one of the symptoms, which need to be considered.

By no means all the consequences are undesirable. Freedom of choice, and a greater range of choice, may create puzzlement, anxiety, and even disorientation, but they are a great deal better than their opposites, compulsion, narrowness and uniformity. The power to be oneself, and choose one's friends, and create one's own world of significance, albeit a limited one, is preferable to the security of some cramping overall system of public meaning and validation. A privatized society can be a society on the move, encouraging individual excellence and giving value to individuality itself. Present-day concern with the value of privacy, and with danger of intrusions on it in a computerized world, is evidence that something of central

3   Bulmer, *Working-Class Images of Society*, p. 23.
4   Gilbert, *The Making of Post-Christian Britain*, p. 97.

human importance is at stake. There are those who criticize privacy in the name of 'openness', 'authenticity' and the 'let it all hang out' syndrome of some over-intensive kinds of fellowship. But those who defend it see the existence of a private world as an essential element in personal autonomy.

Mary Douglas has a rather nice illustration of the point in comparing working-class with some advanced middle-class homes:

> The first thing that is striking about the English working-class home is the attempt to provide privacy in spite of the difficulties of the layout. The respect for the privacy of bodily functions corresponds to the respect for the distinction between social and private occasions; the back of the house is appropriately allocated to cooking, washing and excretory functions; the front parlour, distinguished from the living-room kitchen, is functionless except for public, social representation. Space by no means wasted, it is the face of the house, which speaks composedly and smiles for the rest of the body . . .
>
> Certain families of the middle class tend to break down the barrier between public and private. They seek to live in public together in an unstructured, open room, expressing aptly (perhaps disastrously) their unstructured, personal system of control.[5]

Privatization has religious as well as social strengths. Reference has already been made to the cults which ape family life, but this is by no means the whole story. Daniel Jenkins refers to the inner strengths of Welsh chapels which can seem very private places, shut up tight during the week and with the times of services only occasionally announced. This is not through deliberate secretiveness, but because they 'have come to think of themselves as virtually private affairs, more like families or at least clubs than public institutions open to all'.[6]

Cathedrals invite a different sort of privacy, publicly accessible because anybody can be there, but interior and shut away because 'being there' is all the worshipper has to do. This is perhaps why cathedrals appeal especially to those who live demanding public lives, and who look for private sources of renewal stamped with the kind of public validation a cathedral can supply.

5   Douglas, *Natural Symbols*, p. 191.
6   Daniel Jenkins, *The British: Their Identity and Their Religion* (1975), p. 47.

But the main welcome for the privatization of religion comes from those who reject the public role spelt out for it in the last chapter. The kind of concern expressed there about social cohesion, and the analysis of various manifestations of religion in terms of their functional value, are not popular themes in some quarters. The emphasis is rather on the prophetic impact of a transcendent faith. There are frequent references to the corrupting effect of trying to be socially significant. Better a privatized gospel in its purity than a publicly acceptable religion which has lost its soul.

There are difficulties, though, in being both privatized and prophetic. These will be considered from a theological perspective in the next chapter. Meanwhile the following passage from Berger can serve to pinpoint the sociological difficulties:

> . . . privatized religion is a matter of the 'choice' or 'preference' of the individual or the nuclear family, *ipso facto* lacking in common, binding quality. Such private religiosity, however 'real' it may be to the individuals who adopt it, cannot any longer fulfil the classical task of religion, that of constructing a common world within which all of social life receives ultimate meaning binding on everybody. Instead, this religiosity is limited to specific enclaves of social life that may be effectively segregated from the secularized sectors of modern society. The values pertaining to private religiosity are, typically, irrelevant to institutional contexts other than the private sphere. For example, a business man or politician may faithfully adhere to the religiously legitimated norms of family life, while at the same time conducting his activities in the public sphere without any reference to religious values of any kind.[7]

In other words, a religion which is 'real' only within a particular enclave, has difficulty in moving out of that enclave. A privatized religion may prophesy, but its prophecies are not likely to be heard. Only a church which speaks with the world's voice is likely to be heard by the world; but how can it then escape worldliness?

The problem of the 'reality' of religion is a serious one, and is felt by everybody who has to worship regularly in a largely empty church. Public worship becomes difficult to sustain when numbers fall too low; it begins to *feel* private, and the rows of empty pews

7   Berger, *The Social Reality of Religion*, pp. 132–3.

and the weakly sung hymns are a continual mocking reminder of
its minority status. Credibility, what Berger calls 'plausibility', depends at least in part on the willingness of others to affirm our
beliefs. Reality for us, if we are not to be purely subjective or
idiosyncratic, has to be a shared reality. We test our experiences
against the experiences of others. We talk and read and share each
other's thoughts. We act together in creating a public world of
meaning. But at the very apex of this process, when we most want
to say something about the meaning of life as a whole, about the
universe and our place in it, we have to face the contradiction that
our truth feels private, and can all too easily be dismissed by others
as mere opinion. This is how privatization can erode belief.

The point is a subtle one, and needs to be expressed very carefully
if it is not to be misleading. Membership of even quite a small
group of like-minded people can distract attention from the full
implications of the fact that the world thinks otherwise. Indeed it
can do more than that. Awareness of being different from other
people can in some circumstances reinforce belief rather than erode
it. It was Marx, I think, who said that the Jewish people have
survived, not in spite of anti-Semitism, but because of it. Gilkey, in
the essay already quoted,[8] makes a similar point about the ideals
of the Enlightenment. The only places in the world where they are
still important and creative are among dissident communities in
both East and West; in cultures where they have achieved dominant
power, they are moribund. The same could be said of the churches.
Small is often beautiful. Non-conformity is often more vigorous than
conformity. And Athanasius, the patron saint of nonconformists, is
constantly extolled as a permanent reminder that truth does not
necessarily lie with the big battalions.

Yet what are the grounds for saying that Athanasius, when he
stood out against an Arian world, was right? And what defence is
there against the charge that heresy is always the side which loses
because truth is defined by those who win? The dilemma confront-
ing minority beliefs is a very sharp one, but it seems to me that
there is no future in simply equating vigour with truth, and withdrawing into a private world. On the other hand, the appeal to
reason and evidence as a way of escaping the dilemma immediately
brings the minority making the appeal back into the world of public

8 Gilkey, 'The New Watershed in Theology', p. 23.

discourse, where it is the public criteria of truth which count. To acknowledge this is not to succumb to the view that matters of truth can be decided by a majority vote. It is, however, to cling to the view that matters of truth belong to the public realm where they must be open to public debate. Minorities can, and very properly do, proclaim their own truths, and the degree to which they are accepted is not necessarily a measure of their truth. But unless they are willing to move into the public realm and argue the point, there seems to be no way of distinguishing truth from fantasy.

It is in this rather sophisticated sense that a privatized belief is unstable. The emphasis is on the word 'privatized', which is not the same as 'personal' or 'subjective'. There is a sense, pressed to the limit by Kierkegaard, in which religious truth is essentially subjective. To believe is not to entertain ideas or to come to judicious conclusions. It is to discover subjectively 'what is true for me'. To encounter God is to be grasped, shaken and transformed in one's inmost being. But the proof that this is not merely a private experience is surely to be found in the fact that Kierkegaard spent the whole of his life writing about it. And some of his modern disciples have been no less voluminous.

It is not subjectivity, but the withdrawal into a private world, which makes belief unstable. The dismissal of belief as 'mere opinion', with the implication that one opinion is as good as another, no matter how idiosyncratic it might seem, is probably the most effective present-day disincentive against taking any belief seriously. Why bother to decide between mere opinions? The louder the protagonists shout, and the more distinctive their messages, the more arbitrary the choice appears. If the essence of a pluralist society is that there is no public doctrine which can act as the criterion of truth, then every belief is in some measure undermined.

But the pluralism, as we have seen, is not absolute. There is a world of public discourse, just as there are public issues and broadly shared public values. There is a sense, then, in which involvement by the churches in this public world is an important element in their credibility. To repeat a crucial point already made, this is not to equate truth with popularity, nor is it to look nostalgically to the days when the churches were much more socially significant than they are now. But it *is* to say that belonging to the public world, as well as to a private world, is an inescapable part of the claim that a belief is true.

The argument of the last few pages, though starting with Berger, has to some extent turned his statement on its head. It therefore needs to be asked whether the second part of that statement, to the effect that 'private religiosity' is 'irrelevant to institutional contexts other than the private sphere', may also have to be read the other way round. Does a faith which claims to be more than a private opinion necessarily have to be seen to have implications for public life? It is a question which brings us, by what is perhaps a somewhat unfamiliar route, to the hotly contested issue of Christian involvement in politics.

Peter Hinchliff's 1982 Bampton Lectures on *Holiness and Politics* survey the whole field so admirably that there is no need to do more than restate his main conclusion, and then concentrate on the reactions to it. He argues that there can be no simple passage from Christian principles to political action. This is partly for reasons already familiar, namely the difficulties about consensus in a pluralist society; it is also because the patterns of responsibility in the political sphere are different from and much more complex than those in the private moral sphere. Nevertheless he sees links between them. Politicians are people, and their moral qualities as people constitute the most politically important facts about them. They do not operate in two unrelated spheres, but by the integrity of their own characters they have to try to bridge the gulf between personal idealism and the actualities of political compromise. Too much idealism, too strict an adherence to principles, can be destructive in failing to reckon with the imperfectibility of human nature. Politics, in fact, entails being the best one can and doing the best one can in often unpropitious circumstances.

I am reminded of John Macmurray's description of the State:

> If we track the State to its lair, what shall we find? Merely a collection of overworked and worried gentlemen, not at all unlike ourselves, doing their best to keep the machinery of government working as well as may be, and hard put to it to keep up appearances.[9]

Hinchliff's book was reviewed by Enoch Powell, who dismissed it as 'a brave try', implied that it did not tackle the real religious issue, and concluded his review with these words:

9 John Macmurray, *Persons in Relation* (1961), p. 200.

57

Man the individual is in a permanent and irresolvable tension with man the social animal. He is born as an individual, he dies as an individual, and if there is forgiveness and redemption, he is forgiven and redeemed as an individual. It is to man the individual that the Gospel speaks.[10]

It is important not to misunderstand Powell in this criticism, since he represents in an extreme form a popular type of attack on the churches in Britain for what is seen as an inappropriate, or even scandalous, degree of political involvement. Edward Norman and Peregrine Worsthorne write regularly on the subject, and the following quotations from the latter are fairly typical:

. . . it is only in relation to individuals that Christianity has any clear meaning . . . if the churches don't believe in the primary and absolute importance of the individual Christian, then they know nothing of the Sermon on the Mount . . .[11]

Powell himself, in a different context, disclaims mere individualism:

Without serious exaggeration one might assert that Christianity is not about individuals at all . . . in no sense is society created out of individuals . . . society is the only human reality we know, and the individual is an abstraction in terms of which, for certain purposes, it is convenient or even indispensable to think.[12]

He goes on to describe the Gospel as a 'social gospel', but not in the sense of a 'gospel about secular society. It can only be imparted to the individual as a member of a society . . . its inmost secret is that it is a collective.'

The church, in other words, is a social reality, and it is important to recognize that Powell, unlike perhaps some other commentators, places a high value on it. But it is a social reality apparently unrelated to other social realities, and it is here rather than in what is said about individuals, that we reach the heart of the criticism. For Powell the Gospel is essentially, totally and irreducibly supernatural. The gulf between the natural and the supernatural cannot be crossed by human action, social or otherwise, but only in the church at the eucharist. The cries of pain when the church indulges

10 In *Theology*, vol. LXXXV (1982), pp. 475–6.
11 *Sunday Telegraph*, 25 July 1982.
12 Powell, *Wrestling with the Angel*, pp. 26, 28.

in political activity are not merely the cries of a professional politician who sees amateurs trespassing foolishly in his field, but the
cries of a Christian who sees the one thing which enables him to
escape from the murky realm of political ambiguity, itself being
dragged down into it.

Bruce Reed, from a different perspective, issues the same kind of
warning.[13] The church, in its corporate aspects, must concentrate
on worship, because it is this which gives strength to those actively
engaged in the work of the world to live by the principles of the
Kingdom of God.

But is such a total separation, such a radical removal of the
churches out of the public and into the private realm, either possible
or desirable? The standard answer to Powell's one-sided super-
naturalism is to point to the Incarnation as precisely that which
bridges the gulf, and gives the Gospel its human, social and ultimately political dimensions. His so-called individualism is attacked
on similar grounds. Powell has a valid point, though, in his sometimes perverse interpretations of the New Testament. The Incarnation is not an 'answer' which clarifies the relationship between
divine and human action, but a 'mystery' which opens up new
depths of incomprehension. Man has to wrestle in the dark, like
Jacob with the angel, and the more conscious he is of the mystery
of Christ, the less likely he is to give a Christian label to his political
judgements. There is no quick route from incarnational doctrine to
decisions about the proper relationship between church activity and
political activity.

There may in fact be many ways of relating, appropriate to
different circumstances, and Richard Niebuhr's *Christ and Culture*,
which spells out five of them, is still relevant to the discussion. For
the moment, however, it is the sociological dimension rather than
the theological dimension which is our main concern.

A Powellite church, ministering simply and solely to the inner
lives of individuals, must surely become increasingly unreal and
detached. Powell himself has rightly described the individual as an
'abstraction'. If social studies have achieved anything in the last
hundred years, it has been to demonstrate that human life cannot
be lived or understood apart from its social context. There is no
need to exaggerate this into the error of ascribing everything human

13 Reed, *The Dynamics of Religion*, *passim*.

to the social rather than the individual personal dimension, but the truth is sufficiently obvious to put in question the more extreme forms of emphasis on individual autonomy. As individuals we belong irrevocably to a society, and however we perceive the boundaries of that society, we relate through it to the whole public world.

To acknowledge this is not to diminish the importance and value of individuals as such. Critics of 'socially involved Christians' frequently confuse their concern about the social dimension of life with a lack of concern for the rights and dignities of individuals. But this does not follow. The two concerns need not interfere. Indeed it may be precisely because a particular social set-up is damaging the lives of individuals, that social or political means are sought for changing it.

In short, a Gospel which belongs to the world of public discourse, which it must if it is to be credible, cannot fail to have relevance to public life as well as to private life. To this extent a high degree of social awareness in Christianity is unavoidable. But how ought it to be expressed in Britain today?

A useful first step is to distinguish between a church which breeds politically active Christians, and a church which itself becomes involved in political action. The former is what one ought to expect a healthy church to be doing. The latter can threaten the integrity of the church by attaching ultimate Christian aims to some temporary political programme. If I do not mistake him, this is the broad conclusion reached by Hinchliff.

There is much to be said for it, not least the fact that it is realistic in a way in which much talk about Christian political action is not. Church leaders, and even Synods, may pass unanimous resolutions on a variety of public matters, but even in the most authoritarian church it is rarely true that the church as a whole can speak with one voice. This ought not to be surprising. One of the distinctive marks of the churches ought to be that they draw together human beings across the barriers of class and race and political and every other allegiance, on the basis of a common call and a common status as forgiven sinners. There may be very special occasions when Christian duty is so clear that the only room for doubt is about the quality of Christian commitment. In the Lutheran churches the concept of *status confessionis* (matters on which Christian membership stands or falls) represents this possibility, but it is well recognized how serious a business it is to bind Christian consciences on subjects as fallible as political judgements. In the Church of England, where the boundaries are unclear and broad representativeness is of the essence, the occasion for a *status confessionis* would have to be quite exceptional.

There is a good practical reason, therefore, for wanting to distinguish individual involvement in public affairs from corporate church involvement; the claim that 'the church' is committed to this or that political stance is almost certain to be unreal. Furthermore the cost of stepping into the political arena is high in terms of the distinctive witness of the church as a supernatural body of the kind Powell envisages. Whether or not his argument is accepted at its full force, there is enough truth in it to invite caution. There is also the example of the dire results which follow when political and religious commitment are allowed to reinforce one another. After three weeks of conversations with political and religious leaders in the Middle East, I was left in no doubt that the political problems of the area are made far more intractable by their association with religion.[14] By absolutizing conflicts, and making them a matter of obedience, a politicized religion removes the possibility of compromise. Indeed there is a sense in which all wars are religious wars, in that people will only slaughter each other for something which is felt to be of ultimate significance.[15]

Churches run great risks then if they try as churches to make specific political judgements or take political action. This is not to say that it should never be done. There are times and circumstances when not to do so would be a betrayal, even greater than the betrayal involved in obscuring their distinctive role as witnesses to what lies beyond politics. But the presumption is that in the circumstances of Britain and the British churches today, such occasions are likely to be rare. The involvement, it is constantly said, should be moral rather than political. What does this mean?

The distinction is easier to draw in theory than in practice. Moral pronouncements are at a higher level of generality than political ones, but they can easily seem vacuous unless they are earthed in specific proposals. Furthermore, to make moral judgements entails more than juggling with principles. A moral judgement unrelated to a detailed knowledge of the facts of the case lacks any credibility

14 *Towards Understanding the Arab Israeli Conflict*, p. 98.
15 John S. Dunne, *The City of the Gods* (1965), p. 29 seq.

or moral force. But if it arises out of the kind of knowledge required for making an actual decision, where is the dividing line between morals and politics? Certainly a moralist does not have to take into account the balance of interests or the wheeling and dealing entailed in the political process, but in trying to sort out the moral issues in a matter of public concern, he is likely to have gone a long way down the political road.

Assuming, however, that the distinction can be made, what is the basis of a church's moral contribution to public life in a pluralist society? Much depends on how far the church regards itself merely as a privatized group. The perils of doing this in relation to its claim that the Gospel is true have already been spelt out. In the last resort, it has been argued, truth is public truth. The same considerations surely apply to morality. This is why some at least of the implications of privatization have to be resisted. Private belief is rescued from becoming mere opinion by being brought into the realm of public discourse. In just the same way, morality asserts its character as binding and authoritative by being potentially applicable to all.

This is not an argument for a minority trying to impose its moral standards on an unwilling populace. But it *is* a reason for keeping the discussion of morals firmly within the public framework, looking for new points of contact and agreement, and trying to reinforce such Christian values as are already widely shared. Gordon Dunstan[16] has used the phrase 'the artifice of ethics' to describe the lengthy and elaborate process of fashioning common understandings and obligations. What is true of individuals and groups is even more true of nations. Political ends are not self-evident. The values which undergird a society have to be built slowly into the structure, and from time to time reinforced by being articulated. The fact that all this has to be done against a background of moral disagreement complicates the process but does not invalidate it, any more than differences in belief invalidate the search for truth.

The subject has been much discussed, notably in the famous debate between Lord Devlin and Professor Hart on 'the enforcement of morals'. A single quotation from Lord Devlin is perhaps enough to make the point. Referring to monogamous marriage, he wrote, 'it has got there because it is Christian, but it remains there because

16   G. R. Dunstan, *The Artifice of Ethics* (1974).

it is built into the house in which we live and could not be removed without bringing it down'.[17] The same could be said of other institutions and values, discussed in the previous chapter. Social cohesion and national unity depend on invisible struts and beams, many of which have a strong moral component. Though built into the structure of national life, they cannot be assumed to retain their strength without constant reinforcement. And this is one level on which churches, and no doubt other bodies as well, have an important contribution to make. Unless they make it, the nation could in the end find itself living in a very different kind of house, or even in a row of separate bungalows. And the churches themselves, by accepting a pluralist society's evaluation of their moral teaching as applying only to those who like that sort of thing, would have loosened their own grip on its obligatoriness.

When all this has been said, however, about the refusal to retreat from the public realm, there still remain differences in moral quality as between public and private life. Some of these have already been considered in the light of Weber's list of the qualities required in politicians. Others will be discussed in chapter 10 in relation to a specific public issue. Others, now to be mentioned briefly, form part of an essential reminder that, in politics as much as in personal life, the values making for stability are not the only values which matter.

Dorothy Emmet identifies three strands in social morality which she calls custom, reciprocity and generosity.[18] Sociologists, by and large, concern themselves with custom. My attempt in these first three chapters to use sociological insights in looking at both Church and nation, has almost inevitably veered again and again towards the issue of social cohesion. Custom provides the baseline of morality, the broad rules of thumb and the largely unquestioned assumptions which hold societies together.

Reciprocity has been a major concern of moral philosophers. Discussion of rights and duties, the balancing of mutual interests in the search for fairness, the transcendence of custom in the name of universal moral principles, all these have been the staple diet of rational moral reflection. It is the impersonal ideal of reciprocity

17   Quoted in Basil Mitchell's, *Law, Morality and Religion in a Secular Society* (1967), p. 131. This book takes the Devlin/Hart debate as its starting-point, and provides an excellent introduction to the whole subject of social morality.

18   Emmet, *The Moral Prism*, p. 115 seq.

which has provided objective criteria for judging the *status quo*. The legacy of the Enlightenment, despite the doubts expressed about it, has been one of enormous socio-moral improvement.

But there is also the third element, generosity, which Emmet links specifically with religion. This is the element of personal moral heroism, the contribution made by saints and martyrs. It is the leap of the imagination which enables a familiar moral scene to be viewed in a totally different way. She grounds it in what she calls 'the transcendence of the Good'. Somewhere within the various strands which make up social morality, there has to be 'openness to a possibility which cannot be fully satisfied'.[19] 'Liberty of spirit' is one of the conditions for making bolder moral judgements, a better quality than altruism or disinterestedness, with their somewhat negative flavour. Warmth, appreciation, vision, passion, all these draw their energy from some source beyond ordinary social and intellectual processes.

One of the strengths of privatized religion is its ability to generate such liberty of spirit. One of its weaknesses is its inability to weave it into the other necessary strands in a properly balanced social morality. Unless it does so – and this has been the main argument of this chapter – it runs the risk of losing contact with social reality, and in the end undermining itself. But how in a pluralist society can it be done? Those faced with the practical task of doing the weaving, need to look for help to the theologians.

19   ibid., p. 138.

4

Some Theological Guidelines

One of the tricks of the trade used by social analysts is to present sharp alternatives, and invite a choice between them. There are two possible roads for Christians in a secular pluralist society, we are told, the way of accommodation or the way of resistance. The churches can either allow themselves to take on the shape and role dictated to them by the needs of the secular world, or they can accept the full implications of their minority status, and resolutely 'do their own thing'.

Gilbert summarizes the dilemma and its consequences in these terms:

> Accommodation is not the only possible response to the emergence of a post-Christian culture. But in the last resort there is but one alternative: the lonely sectarian road of resistance. Secularization, in short, is beginning to polarize Christians into camps so far apart, so dissimilar, that in the future all other alignments and differences may become not just secondary, but irrelevant.[1]

Neither alternative is attractive. I have argued in the previous chapters that a church which cuts itself off from the world of public discourse loses credibility, and that a nation which allows this to happen to its churches may threaten its own stability. On the other hand, a church which fails to maintain its distinctness from the society in which it is set, or to swim against the secular currents of its day, becomes complacent and corrupt and ultimately sub-Christian. It is an old dilemma, sharpened by the pressures of secularization, but not created by them, and through most of their history many of the churches have been adept at finding a middle road

1 Gilbert, *The Making of Post-Christian Britain*, p. 133.

65

between the two extremes. Some of the practical ways in which this is done, or might be done, will form the theme of later chapters. Our immediate task in this chapter is to explore the kind of help theology might give in steering an appropriate course.

But first there is a fundamental problem to be faced. Before looking for theological guidance, it has to be asked what kind of theology is possible in a secular pluralist society.

In a supermarket there can be no clearly defined 'best buy'. Nor is there any way of deciding what the word 'best' could mean in that context. The essence of supermarket shopping is that customers buy what they perceive as 'best for them', given their particular needs, backgrounds and tastes. Choices, in other words, are relative to the circumstances of the chooser.

The analogy is a crude one, but it serves to illustrate the link between pluralism in beliefs and relativism in theology. In a world where different beliefs are seen to be on offer, and where different people have good reasons for choosing differently, the claim to possess some final absolute version of truth is fatally weakened. Truth is relativized.

Like the dilemma already mentioned, this is not a new insight. People have long since ceased to be surprised that the majority of Arabs are Muslims, or the majority of Indians Hindus, or the majority of English public schoolboys Church of England. The idea that people's perceptions of truth depend on who they are and where they have come from seems the merest commonsense. What the pressures of secularization have done, however, aided by the growth during the last century or so of greater historical and socio-logical consciousness, is to sharpen the sense of relativity to the point at which it becomes central to the theological agenda.

Sociology is relativistic by nature. To study human behaviour in its social context is to work on the assumption that different contexts give rise to different patterns of behaviour. When sociological meth-ods are applied to religious belief, and when societies themselves are seen as human constructions which set the conditions of belief, then the human relativistic elements in belief become all too ob-vious. This goes beyond the mere observation that different beliefs are found in different societies. It offers an explanation of why some beliefs appear plausible in some contexts, while others do not. In so doing it strikes at the root of the religious claim to be able to say something of permanent and universal significance about ultimate truth. Berger puts the point succinctly. Sociological understanding

> offers an *explanation* of belief that divests the specific case of its uniqueness and authority. The mystery of faith now becomes scientifically graspable, practically repeatable, and generally applicable . . . The community of faith is now understandable as a *constructed entity* – it has been constructed in a specific human history, by human beings.[2]

Berger goes on to suggest that this is by no means the whole story; but before looking at the more positive side, it is important to face the full implications of the relativistic viewpoint. They are not confined to theology. Many natural scientists have been surprised to find in recent years the extent to which sociologists of knowledge have undermined ordinary commonsense scientific claims about the objectivity of their results. If a certain type of explanation is acceptable, or a certain type of experiment is done, because these fit with the general assumptions of a particular society, the notion of scientific truth begins to take on a very different complexion. In fact after listening to much criticism of this kind at a huge world conference of scientists and theologians, I wrote an essay with the deliberately provocative title, 'Can Science Survive?'[3] My main theme was that science and theology are under exactly the same pressures in a world where politicized interpretations of so-called 'objectivity' are becoming increasingly popular, especially in Third World countries. Scientists and theologians ought, therefore, to see that they have a common interest in defending the notion of some ultimate, even if unattainable, truth. To succumb too completely to relativism is to find oneself on a very slippery slope indeed.

The same is true in the moral sphere. A relativistic morality has lost the very thing which makes a moral demand feel obligatory. If something is right it ought, at least in principle, to be right for everybody. Even Situation Ethics, which pushed to its extreme limit the idea that individual choices belong wholly to particular contexts, depended on the assertion of at least one ultimate and universal principle – the law of love.

2   Peter L. Berger, *A Rumour of Angels* (1969), p. 54.
3   In J. M. Turner (ed.), *Queen's Essays* (1980).

It is small wonder that the churches have on the whole shied away from the consequences of relativism, while making various internal adjustments to reduce its impact. Popular language about there being 'many roads to God' implicitly acknowledges the problem, but is usually not pressed to the point at which its effect on traditional Christian belief begins to be felt. Anglican claims to comprehensiveness can often amount to no more than this general kind of open-mindedness. More sectarian churches, on the other hand, ignore the problem by not allowing it to intrude. At the extreme end of the sectarian scale, where little groups believe that they possess the final and absolute truth, relativism is not an issue at all. Provided one keeps the barriers round one's church high enough, there is really no more to be said.

Roman Catholicism provides an interesting example of a church which has gone a long way towards mitigating the problem by distinguishing between primary and secondary truths. Its internationalism forces it to acknowledge many different styles of being Roman Catholic, each of them deeply influenced by its cultural setting. Even in Britain the differences between Irish Roman Catholicism and traditional upper-class English Papism are strikingly obvious. Yet these are held together by a framework of teaching which appears on the surface to be much more monolithic than it is in practice. A high degree of relativism is acknowledged, but it is a relativism which is not felt to touch the central faith or institutions of the church, and so does not imperil its essential unity.

But is it possible to stop short at cultural differentiation, while still making absolute theological claims? My own belief is that it is not. Relativism has to be tackled head-on at the very centre of the Christian faith, in the claims made about God himself.

The essential step in doing so is to recognize that, if all truth is relative, then the fact that we *know* this implies that there is at least one respect in which we are able to transcend relativity.

It is a very simple step, and it is one that is applicable in many fields of study which seem at first sight to reduce human beings to mere products of the forces being studied, whether physical, biological, psychological or social. In the end our full humanity always eludes these descriptions because it is human beings who are doing the describing. Unless in some way we transcend our description of ourselves, that description itself must be seen as a mere product of our circumstances. The sociological theories which relativize our beliefs are themselves relative to the particular sociological milieu in which they are put forward. Berger has used the phrase 'relativizing the relativizers'.[4] In an equally striking and well-known phrase, he has recommended the search for 'signals of transcendence', which can point the way out of the relativistic straitjacket.

One theologian who has pursued this line of thought with commendable rigour is Don Cupitt. The fact that some of his later writings have lost their grip on the notion of God's transcendent reality, largely under the influence of Cupitt's own curiously dogmatic version of positivism, should not diminish respect for his earlier work, and for his resoluteness in trying to face the problems. His book *The Leap of Reason*[5] is a powerful argument for the view that religious knowledge, knowledge of God and man as spirit, does provide a means of escaping the ultimate consequences of relativism. It is as we know our imprisonment that we can begin in spirit to transcend it.

> By 'spirituality' I mean our reflexive ability to transcend ourselves by becoming aware of and by being able to criticize and even change our own fundamental patterns of thought. We are in spirit in so far as we can *change our minds*, in the strongest sense of that phrase . . . it is manifest in *humour*, as when one must transcend oneself spiritually in order to see that the joke is on oneself; it is manifest in *repentance*, when one both affirms and transcends the self that one has been hitherto; it is manifest in *iconoclasm*, when someone overthrows socially accepted religious symbols; and it is manifest in *conversion* of every kind.[6]

What we can thus experience in ourselves is reflected in God's dealings with us. To know God is to transcend every representation of God. The crucial distinction is between what Cupitt calls 'God-in-the-programme', i.e. knowledge of God as expressed within a particular religious tradition, and the God who is pure transcendent spirit.

> If in religion the negative way has precedence over the affirmative way, if the possibility of a mystical transcendence of programmatic religion is kept in view . . . then that religion is spiritual

---

4 Berger, *A Rumour of Angels*, ch. 2.
5 Don Cupitt, *The Leap of Reason* (1976).
6 Don Cupitt, in *Theology*, LXXVIII (1975), pp. 297, 299.

. . . God absolute, God as pure spirit, can be expressed only by insisting upon the relativity of even the most comprehensive and powerful religious programme . . .

Cupitt's reference to 'the negative way' is a reminder that what is being said here has respectable theological antecedents in Orthodoxy as well as in the mystical tradition of the West. The so-called 'Apophatic Way' in Orthodox theology, whereby God is known primarily through what he is not, primarily through denials that any merely human description can encompass him, was not conceived as a response to external pressures, but arose out of profound meditation on what it means for God to be God. What is important for our purposes about Cupitt's approach and what carries some theological risks, is his attempt to use the negative way to meet the challenge of twentieth-century pluralism. This is where his phrase 'God-in-the-programme' needs careful attention and is helpfully fleshed out by John Bowker to whom we shall turn in a minute. The point is that the God who is disclosed to us as we acknowledge our relativity, is not necessarily to be known through all the disconnected bits and pieces and half-baked ideas which float around in a pluralist society. The great religious traditions have their own integrity, their own inner consistencies, and their own means of testing themselves against reality. They are the validated stepping-stones to God. But as systems they only bring us to God-in-the-programme. It is when we see their relativity, when we see *them* as human constructions providing no more than the setting for God to disclose himself, that we touch the hem of the transcendent. Though we only know in part, and though all knowledge will vanish away, the knowledge is not thereby rendered otiose. To see that it is not sufficient, is not to repudiate it. The story that Thomas Aquinas came to realize that all his voluminous systematic theology was 'but straw', is not an excuse for ignoring it. There are well-tried ways to God, but the only way to know God *as God* is to come to terms with their relativity.

A corollary of all this is that the sectarian solution to the problems of pluralism and relativism is in the end seen to be no solution at all. A God who has to be protected from iconoclasm by the erection of high barriers around a particular expression of the faith, has already moved a long way in the direction of becoming an idol. The barriers may be barriers of ecclesiastical exclusiveness, but they can also be theological. In some sectarian circles, for instance, highly specialized theologies can give an air of respectability to what are in fact closed systems of thought.[7] The various fundamentalisms fall into this category. To move into such a system, to put oneself beyond the possibility of criticism or refutation, is in the end to give supreme value to a human construction, however impressive its divine imprint. The modern vogue for so-called 'creation science' in America, which employs a dazzling array of spurious arguments against orthodox evolutionary theory, decked out with apparently meticulous scholarship, is a particularly striking example of this phenomenon.[8]

This criticism of sectarianism applies even more strongly to less coherent forms of belief. The accusation often made against a relativistic approach to theology, that it can open the door too wide, and give equal credence to almost anything, is not valid against Cupitt, or against the approach outlined here. Let me stress once again that the 'programme', to use Cupitt's terminology, which has to be transcended, must itself form part of the public world in which assertions of truth are tested by ordinary rational means.

But if the head-on approach to relativism can yield important insights into the character of the knowledge of God, it has to be admitted that it also creates problems – problems which lend attractiveness to the sectarian alternative. In what sense, for instance, can any faith be distinctive if all faiths are relative? What becomes of Christian claims to finality? And what about authority?

These are huge questions, to which I shall attempt to sketch out at least a partial answer in chapter 9. Meanwhile let me give a clue to that answer by returning to John Bowker. His two volumes of Wilde lectures[9] explore the way in which what he calls 'the sense of God' develops and expresses itself through different types of human experience and in different religious traditions. The actual form which these expressions and traditions take depends in part on their own internal logic, in part on the accidents or providences of history, and in part on their ability to deal with the actual crises

7   Robert Towler and A. P. M. Coxon, *The Fate of the Anglican Clergy* (1979), p. 203.
8   Philip Kitcher's, *Abusing Science: The Case Against Creationism* (1982) provides an excellent summary of the debate.
9   John Bowker, *The Sense of God* (1973) and *The Religious Imagination and the Sense of God* (1978).

and limitations faced by human beings. Some traditions die. All traditions from time to time go through 'crises of plausibility' when they are no longer found by their adherents to provide adequate explanations or to be 'life-enhancing'. But creative transformations are possible, transformations marked by a kind of eloquent silence. Bowker's method is to look 'with some care at people overwhelmed by the impossibility of prevailing characterizations of God, who yet, reduced to the desperation of their own silence, heard the word made flesh within them speak once more'.[10] This is not far from Cupitt's God-in-the-programme, who has to be transcended.

Where Bowker goes further than Cupitt is in his sympathetic exploration of the integrity of separate religious traditions. *Within* each tradition the questions of distinctiveness, finality and authority do not arise. The way prescribed is the right way for those who go along it, and if a particular way has limitations, these are more likely to be seen in their true character by those who belong to that way, than by those who criticize it from outside. If there is to be any meeting point in 'the sense of God', and here I go beyond Bowker, it is not to be found in vague religious indifferentism, but among those who have taken seriously the integrity of their own tradition, and have faced its relativity, and have thus transcended it.

Christians have a special reason for welcoming this approach to theology, as Tillich pointed out a quarter of a century ago.[11] A faith whose central symbol is the cross can scarcely avoid facing the lack of ultimacy of all concrete religious expressions. It is founded on a paradox. The one who was seen to be the Way, the Truth and the Life only revealed his full glory in rejection and death. The one whom the disciples thought they knew, told them that it was expedient for them that he should go away. Christians are told to die daily, and this dying to self includes dying to ideas about the self and its own pretentious claims. Other faiths may have other ways of representing this paradoxical element in religious commitment. I am not sufficiently well informed to know. But it seems to me that one of the great strengths of cross-centred Christianity is that it positively invites this double movement – of faith in the tradition, and acknowledgment of the inadequacy of the tradition – which

10   ibid. (1978) p. 316.
11   Paul Tillich, *The Dynamics of Faith* (1957), p. 97.

72

opens the way for the disclosure of God. In the Resurrection we know the mystery of God's presence through, not despite of, the very processes which worked to deny, distort and destroy him.

Another less dramatic way of making the same point, and one which brings us closer to the practical questions underlying this chapter, is to reflect on how theology can help to give meaning to human experiences. On a simple view it might be supposed that in a society with a strong religious tradition meanings are simply 'read off' from experiences in the light of some predetermined scheme. A death, for example, might be seen as a punishment, or a warning, or a sign of evil forces at work, or as the natural climax to a life, depending on the circumstances and the prevailing theology. No doubt in some societies this is the way things happen, and when Berger writes about religion protecting people from meaninglessness, the implication seems to be that this is how they ought to happen.[12]

There is an alternative model, however, and one which seems to do more justice to the creative role of theology. According to this model the discovery of meaning arises out of wrestling and conflict between the religious tradition and what is actually being experienced. It is a discovery, a disclosure, not a mere application of some truth already known. When Job agonized over his sufferings his friends, far from failing him, offered him the summary of a religious tradition which was both profound and helpful. Job had to reject it, and come to terms in his own way with the nature of God as expressed in it, because the meaning which alone could satisfy him had to be received from God himself. God himself had to answer him – and did. God's answer, in his disclosure of himself, and Job's response, prepare the way for the distinctive Christian understanding of revelation. 'I have heard of thee by the hearing of the ear, but now mine eye seeth thee. Wherefore I abhor myself and repent in dust and ashes.'[13] What the book represents God as saying is not essentially different from much of what had already been said by Job's friends. It is the fact that there is an answer at all, a coming of God to man, which discloses God at a depth which is inaccessible through mere acceptance of the tradition from the lips of others.

It is at the intersections of life, the meeting points between trad-

12 David Martin (ed.), *Sociology and Theology: Alliance and Conflict* (1980), pp. 155–8.
13 Job 42:5–6.

ition and experience, or between apparently incompatible traditions, in the moments of disorder, anxiety, pain, incomprehension,
inadequacy, when the soul cries out to God, that the struggle to
find meaning can be most rewarding. This is why a complacent
faith is unrevealing, and a faith protected against exposure to the
contradictions of experience becomes in the end idolatrous.

The same principle seems to apply in the moral sphere. In the
book already quoted, Dorothy Emmet makes the point that moral
conflict is not an unfortunate occurrence, but is central to moral
discovery. It is rarely that a single factor in a given set of circumstances points the way unequivocally towards what ought to be
done. Actual decisions emerge out of a complex of purposes, principles and feelings all of which have to be considered. It would be
ideal, she says, if our moral judgements were like 'white light showing clearly what action would be best in any situation'; but in
practice,

> just as light coming through a prism is refracted into a spectrum
> of different colours, so our moral thinking shows us a range of
> different features, and attention can fasten now on one and now
> on another. And just as it is absurd to maintain that one colour
> in the spectrum is the only true, or even the truest form of light,
> so we must not make the mistake of assuming that one feature in
> the moral spectrum is the only true form of morality.[14]

It is only as this problematic character of morality is faced, that
it can have authority.

> The full stringency of morality is realized when one sees both
> that one's judgement is problematic and that one must take
> responsibility for it. It may indeed be that morality can only be
> final if it is allowed to be problematic, not given in absolute
> principles. The transcendental reference in the Sovereignty of
> Good can put a question mark against the finality of any purpose,
> however imperious, and the universal applicability of any prin-
> ciple, however imperative.[15]

Finality, in other words, belongs to the transcendent, where alone
it can be truly final. To admit the relativity of all merely human

14 Emmet, *The Moral Prism*, p. 1.
15 ibid., p. 145.

formulations is the most profound way of acknowledging the ultimate authority of God. If this sounds unattractive to those who like their morality to come with plain authoritative labels, it is worth remembering the moral enigmas in the teachings of Jesus. There seems to be an extraordinary misconception, at least among those who write angry letters to bishops, that the teaching of Jesus was simple.[16] In fact he very rarely gave a straight answer to a straight question. This was not because he was evasive, but because his prime purpose was to open up for the questioner a new moral and religious dimension. He was doing, in fact, what Dorothy Emmet describes.

This chapter began by setting out the contrast between two possible policies for the churches in this country – accommodation to the prevailing culture, or resistance to it. If the theological position outlined here is sound, it supports the view that neither alternative is acceptable, but that it is precisely in the tension between them that Christians will find their truest relationship with God. Martin writes about the constant tension in Christianity through being 'a carrier of rationality, bureaucracy and disenchantment', i.e. part of a modern secular society, '*and* their critic in the name of transcendence and mystery'.[17] In an earlier part of the same essay[18] he makes the point that Christianity with its strong emphasis on interior individual choice, constantly has to strain against the pull of nature, in contrast with Judaism which reinforces natural community tendencies. Jews can be born Jews, whereas Christians have to be born again. There is always a sense, therefore, in which Christians are at odds with their environment, and find themselves pushed in the direction of privatization. But to allow this to happen, to allow the emphasis on choice to become too prominent, runs the risk of destroying the base from which it began. Christianity thus finds itself in perpetual tension between minorities who try to take the principle of choice to its limits, and the majority who conserve the tradition, but at the cost of losing interiority and spontaneity.

Individual Christians cannot possibly represent all such tensions within themselves. Most people settle for a simple faith, and rightly

16 The point is well made in an essay by John Tinsley, 'Tell it Slant', in *Theology* LXXXIII (1980), pp. 163–70.
17 Martin, *The Dilemmas of Contemporary Religion*, p. 54.
18 ibid., p. 30 seq.

so. But a church can and must represent the tensions, both in its official teachings and in the variety of people, roles and experiences for which it caters. One of the dangers faced by churches in a pluralist society is that they can lose the incentive to hold this variety together. Different groups with different interests can simply drift away from one another, in the direction of greater privatization, thereby forfeiting their ability to correct one another, and ultimately forfeiting their credibility.

By contrast, the opportunity presented to churches by a pluralist society is that it allows different traditions to develop and maintain their own inner integrity, and by interacting fruitfully, to transcend their own relativity. I shall be suggesting in chapter 6 that one of the other fruits of this interaction may be a readiness to share some common sense of responsibility for the society to which they belong. This can be important for them in keeping them in what I have called 'the world of public discourse', and important for the society in helping to maintain its cohesion.

The need for correctives and counter-influences for traditionalists and dissenters, for conservatives and radicals, is obvious wherever one looks in the life of the churches. Dissent needs something to dissent from, and itself gradually becomes absorbed back into tradition.[19] Small committed groups and new movements can be sources of new life; they can also become over-intensive, oppressive and even demonic.[20] Tradition can become a dead weight if it is absorbed unreflectingly; if deliberately chosen, its resources can add an essential element of depth to the spiritual life. Radicalism can give spiritual strength by forcing churches to face facts in the secular world; it can also become so conformed to the secular world as to be indistinguishable from it.

Such contrasts are easy to spell out on paper, and very difficult to live out in practice. The unity of a church within itself, not to mention its relationship with other churches and other religious traditions, is bound to be a complex business if the various tensions and balances are to be preserved. There is no formula which can include them, and no single pattern which is right for all times and circumstances. The chapters which follow will attempt to explore some of the implications of this complexity in terms of practical

19   Jenkins, *The British*, pp. 108–9.
20   Hinchliff, *Holiness and Politics*, p. 56.

questions facing the Church of England. The final word in this chapter, however, must be a reminder that Christians ought not to be surprised at the complex character of the goal. It is surely one of the implications of a Trinitarian theology that unity should be seen to have many dimensions.

5

Folk Religion

From a sociological perspective active churchgoers form the tip of a huge religious iceberg. They are simply the most visible and articulate part of a much more widespread phenomenon.

From the perspective of some of the churchgoers themselves the picture looks quite different. For them there is a clear dividing-line between 'committed believers', and those who enjoy various degrees of half-faith or non-faith as measured by the believers' standards of religious orthodoxy. Far from resting on a massive sub-stratum, a true faith has to separate itself from dangerous and distracting substitutes.

Any study and evaluation of folk religion, therefore, runs into difficulties at the very start. The use of the term can seem pejorative to some, a piece of self-definition by believers, which arrogantly separates off the second-class religious citizens, and confusing to others, who find it hard to recognize that what is described has clear links with religion as they experience it. In adopting a broad sociological perspective in this chapter, I do not want to prejudge the theological issue which underlies this distinction. We shall return to it at the end. It will be obvious, though, that a theology which takes relativism seriously will be more inclined to look sympathetically at a wide range of religious phenomena, than one which claims to have exclusive possession of ultimate truth.

The term 'folk religion' itself is one of a number used to describe various aspects of something so amorphous that a single clear definition is impossible. I use it here, in an English setting and with experience of ministry in the Church of England particularly in mind, as a general term for the unexpressed, inarticulate, but often deeply felt, religion of ordinary folk who would not usually describe themselves as church-going Christians yet feel themselves to have some sort of Christian allegiance.

Wider definitions are possible, and other terms can usefully supplement this meaning, but since my concern is mainly practical I intend to concentrate on those who see themselves as having some relationship, however tenuous, with the main-line Christian churches. These are the people who bring their children for baptism and want to be married and buried in church, and describe themselves on forms as C. of E., and who would be offended if they were described as un-Christian. Some of the outward signs of allegiance may be disappearing, but the evidence for a basic religiousness in human beings, even in a secular age, remains strong.

Greeley, writing from an American perspective, claims that 'basic human religious needs and basic religious functions have not changed very notably since the late Ice Age'.[1] For him the modern 'crisis of religion' exists only in university campuses. The patterns of life and belief of ordinary people persist over extraordinary periods of time. Martin[2] and Towler have made similar claims for the persistence of English religiousness, and the proportion of those who still in some way or another identify themselves with the churches remains astonishingly high compared with the number who actually attend.

Towler[3] uses the phrase 'common religion' to describe, not only the underground religion of common people which survived the processes of Christianization in Europe, but also the curious amalgam of ideas which compose the faith of many of those in the churches. He doubts whether there was ever a time when 'official belief' touched more than a tiny minority. Intellectuals may find it hard to credit that otherwise sensible people are helped by notions of luck, fate, astrology, etc., but the evidence is that they are, and that what the vast majority of people actually believe, as opposed to what they profess in church circles to believe, is by official standards bizarre.

Richard Hoggart[4] wrote about the 'primary religion' of his childhood with its emphasis on decency, a basic morality, rites of passage, and its suspicion of too much overt religiousness, and the pattern he describes is still visible in working-class communities

1 Andrew M. Greeley, *Unsecular Man: The Persistence of Religion* (1972), p. 1.
2 Martin, *A Sociology of English Religion, passim.*
3 R. Towler, *Homo Religiosus* (1974), p. 147 seq.
4 Richard Hoggart, *The Uses of Literacy* (1957), pp. 93–9.

today, certainly in the North of England. 'Civic religion' is another variation on the same theme, though here the emphasis is on public occasions – the kind of rituals from inaugurating a new mayor to singing hymns at football matches – which serve to strengthen the sense of community identity.[5] There is also a phrase 'implicit religion' used by some as an omnibus term to cover all forms of religiousness apart from the explicit religion of the churches.

I shall stick to the phrase 'folk religion', while recognizing these other nuances, because it is the one most commonly in use among church members. Examples of it are legion.

The Smith family are not church attenders, but Mrs Smith was baptized in infancy at St Mary's and feels, now she has a son of her own, that he should be baptized there too. When the vicar explains that such a baptism would be meaningless because her own baptism has apparently meant nothing to her, she is deeply offended and writes to the bishop:

> Mr K. has not changed his mind and feels it would be hypocritical of him to baptise my son. I feel that his pompous and arrogant attitude towards me is not that of a minister of God. I could no more bare my soul to him than to the devil. This is what really appals and disgusts me, that a man who is a vicar can look at an innocent babe and say, 'No, I will not baptize you; go somewhere else.' This is not a direct quote from Mr K., but as far as I am concerned this is what it amounts to.[6]

The strength of the emotion is obvious. From Mr K.'s point of view it all looks very different. He feels he wants to preserve the integrity of his role as a priest, and comments; 'When anyone doesn't get their own way, it is not uncommon for them to resort to vitriolic attack.' He too is deeply involved emotionally.

Controversies over weddings, funerals and even over gravestones can reveal the same emotional intensity, but there is evidence that some of these focal points of meaning and emotion are changing their character. Mourning rituals, for example, are becoming more perfunctory. There can be a good deal of embarrassment about handling traumatic experiences in circles where Christian ritual has itself become a source of anxiety rather than a help in carrying the

5   R. J. Bocock, 'Ritual: Civic and Religious' in *British Journal of Sociology* (1970), 21, pp. 285–97.
6   Actual letter.

emotions. A recent study on the meaning of rites of passage for different age groups[7] has revealed that for the younger unchurched group, the most significant turning point in life was not marriage but the acquisition of a mortgage. It was this, rather than any religious ritual, which was seen as marking the transition to adult responsibility. In the same way the birth of a first child was the most significant factor in changing social relationships. It is possible, therefore, that the specifically liturgical element in folk religion may be on the wane, indeed in some urban areas it has virtually disappeared. But the need for some kind of quasi-religious markers to give shape and meaning to life, may persist even when the traditional ways of doing this are no longer felt to be relevant.

Meanwhile among those for whom liturgy still has resonances, liturgical revision has aroused as much emotion as rigid baptismal policies. The following extracts from two letters are typical of those received when I was in the firing line as chairman of the committee publishing the Alternative Service Book. The first was written on Remembrance Day and, though incoherent, brings together in a highly characteristic fashion many of the basic themes of English folk religion:

> In remembering our many men and boys who went into battle with the prayers on their lips and comfort they received from the wonderful and beautiful words of comfort they got from their Prayer Books they carried, I know this from personal experience . . . many of them know their prayers, being taught at the knees of their grandparents and parents with comfort of the beautiful words. This could not happen today, I refer to the so-called new hymn and prayer books. Never has anything in our church history caused so much misery. Everything in them is just mumbo jumbo.

War experience, family continuity, stability in a changing world, cluster round a form of words which seem to symbolize them. The second letter is a cri-de-coeur from *The Times*, which illustrates the same theme of security. The church needs to be *there*, and preferably unchanging, as a foil for a life to be lived mostly outside it.

7 F. Musgrove and R. Middleton, 'Rites of Passage and the Meaning of Age in Three Contrasted Social Groups' in *British Journal of Sociology* (1981) *32*, pp. 39–54.

When I was young the church was like a mother, a centre of activity, full of security and warmth, and as one grew older it was natural to feel one could survive quite well without her, returning rapidly in time of trouble or insecurity or love. Whatever one's views about the new services, the change is, to say the least, mistimed, since many people wishing to return to the church in these insecure times are finding themselves alienated by it. Personally the new services make one feel aggressive . . .

This is a classic example of the sort of religious phenomenon described by Bruce Reed. The oscillation between dependence on the church and freedom from it, between worship and work, fits exactly the theory mentioned briefly on page 48.

Reed has interesting things to say about folk religion, seeing it as an aberration from this normal process of oscillation. The folk religionist, instead of using religious symbolism as a means of handling religious needs and growing through them, gets stuck on the symbols themselves. Words, rituals, buildings, become more important than the meaning they symbolize. What matters in terms of folk religion is that the ritual should be 'done properly', and when done properly in satisfaction of an immediate need, it carries no further implications. Baptism, for instance, may satisfy an immediate need to give significance to the birth of a child, or perhaps even just to satisfy grandmother's insistence that family tradition should be preserved. But that is all, and arguments by clergymen about commitment and responsibility carry no weight. The religious process, in Reed's terminology, the cycle of renewal and growth, has been frustrated, the symbol leads nowhere, and the folk religionist is locked into his ritual in a way which is ultimately sterile.

These are harsh criticisms, but they echo the experience of many clergy in dealing with the rather limited group of people who still want to make use of religious rituals in this way. Reed has himself been criticized for a treatment of symbols which seems to suppose that meaning can somehow be detached from them. In fact meaning and symbols develop in complex interrelationship. A ritual may not mean the same for the person who is undergoing it as for the clergyman who is performing it, but it undoubtedly *has* a meaning, and one which has grown, perhaps deviously, out of the religious tradition. It may, therefore, be more fruitful to explore what the different meanings are, than to condemn an attitude to the ritual simply because it does not conform to official expectations.

Reed has also been criticized for psychologizing a phenomenon which has much deeper anthropological roots than the examples so far mentioned might lead one to suppose. Gustav Mensching in an early essay on the subject[8] pointed out that folk beliefs are remarkably similar in different parts of the world. Like Greeley with his reference to the Ice Age, he was impressed by the sheer persistence of the traditional communities in which such beliefs flourish, and which Greeley sees as being supplemented by, rather than replaced by, more modern forms of association. Old patterns of life survive, even in unlikely places, and old beliefs and rituals with them. In Mensching's words: 'The primitive ancient experiences of mankind are everywhere the same, and later men for the most part never transcend them.'

Does this mean that the roots of folk religion are ultimately pagan? Visser 'T Hooft writing out of his European experience, with Hitler's religion of blood, soil and race in mind, has no doubt that Europe has faced, and to some extent still is facing, the recrudescence of an alternative religion.[9] Neo-paganism, as he calls it, is not a precursor to Christianity, still less the submerged part of a Christian iceberg, but a dangerous opponent. To think otherwise is to fall into the error of imagining that in a secularized world any kind of religion is better than atheism or agnosticism. In Renan's words, 'The gods only go away to make places for other gods.' And the 'other gods' may be demonic.

The relationship between basic human religiosity, primitive paganism, which may still be expressing itself in folk religion, and the much more sinister neo-paganism, obviously needs careful study. Examples have already been given of the way in which frustrated religious impulses quickly generate anger. In fact one of the most striking features of the whole phenomenon is the amount of emotion capable of being released. It is as well to reckon with the fact, therefore, that the road from frustrated and misplaced civic religion to the barbarities of the National Front and its successors, may be uncomfortably short.

8 G. Mensching, 'The Masses, Folk Belief and Universal Religion' (1947) quoted in Schneider (1964), p. 273.
9 W. A. Visser 'T. Hooft, 'Evangelism among Europe's Neo-Pagans' in International Review of Mission (1977), pp. 349–60.

Basic to an understanding of folk religion is the recognition that it is expressing a real need deeply rooted in human nature. The fact that it is non-doctrinal, and in many respects non-rational, is a hidden advantage to its practitioners rather than a defect, because part of the need may be to escape from the exclusiveness of 'orthodoxy'. Orthodox religion maps out an area of doctrinal soundness, and puts barriers around it. Those who are not part of this process are apt to reject it as something done by somebody else, and the more professionally it is done, the more instinctive the rejection is likely to be. In his fascinating account of religious attitudes during the First World War, which has much to say about folk religion, Alan Wilkinson remarks,

> The readiness of both troops and those at home to believe in supernatural deliverances, to trust in superstition or fatalism, illustrates the fact that English people will often readily believe in the supernatural, provided it is not part of the Bible or the institutionalized supernaturalism of the church.[10]

Some of the same impulses may be at work in the remarkable popularity of the cults of unreason among university undergraduates. A study done in 1979 reported that some 50 per cent of those asked had quasi-religious beliefs about spacemen visiting the earth and other oddities, well outside the ambit of orthodox science or religion.[11] A more recent study on school-children reveals even greater confusion between space fiction and theology, with Christ interpreted as an alien from another world.

Part of the attraction of such beliefs seems to lie precisely in the fact that they are not orthodox. They seem to be a step on the road to personal discovery, a do-it-yourself religion. There is a need, in other words, to be oneself, to belong to one's own culture and community, and not simply to accept what is handed down from above.

There are also some particular needs, some of which have been mentioned already, to mark significant moments in life, to express family solidarity (maybe by doing what 'Gran' wants in having one's child baptized), to belong somewhere, and to feel that there

10 Alan Wilkinson, *The Church of England and the First World War* (1978), p. 195.
11 A. Hammerton and A. C. Downing, 'Fringe Belief among Undergraduates' in *Theology* (1979) LXXXII, pp. 433–6.

is some ultimate source of meaning and security. After all, 'we must be here for a purpose'.[12]

The fact that these needs, when brought into contact with the churches, express themselves in ways which do not conform to the expectations of those asked to meet them, is for some clergy an acute source of conflict. They may feel they are being pushed into a role which they do not like, and which threatens the integrity of their message. 'I was not ordained to decorate civic occasions or to prostitute the sacraments for those who do not believe in them.' In a time when clerical identity itself is under strain, and when clergy feel more and more marginal to society, there is an understandable dislike of being 'used' by those who are felt basically not to care. There are also serious theological and liturgical objections against using services clearly designed for committed believers in contexts where the commitment is, to say the least, doubtful. Liturgical revision has introduced new emphases into the Church of England, not all of which may be desirable.

I became aware, however, of the extent to which theological conviction can hide other motives, after long discussions and correspondence with a priest who wanted to resign from his working-class parish, because he could no longer justify theologically the kind of things he was required to do. Infant baptism was a particular source of theological perplexity, but it was the strong folk religion element in the parish as a whole which finally led to his resignation. Three years later, when he was considering a return to the parochial ministry in a much more middle-class environment, he said to me in reflecting on his previous experience, 'It wasn't a question of theology at all. It was my inability to accept my own alienation from a working-class culture.' This was said by a man who had been a life-long middle-class member of the Labour Party, and who in the light of his ideals had found it too painful to face the truth about himself. In a middle-class parish his theological scruples disappeared, largely because he now found he could understand the needs being expressed by the people, and so could handle them in ways which did not threaten his integrity.

It is important, of course, not to psychologize away what remains a serious theological problem. Gilbert has an interesting account of early Protestant attempts to create 'a world of virtuoso Christians'.[13]

12 Hoggart, *The Uses of Literacy*, p. 95.
13 Gilbert, *The Making of Post-Christian Britain*, p. 28 seq.

With the rejection of monasticism and clericalism as symbols of a specially high degree of Christian commitment, the choice lay between retiring into a ghetto or trying to sanctify the masses. Wesley's mission was 'to spread Scriptural holiness across the land'. 'To aim so high', comments Gilbert, 'was to raise also the price of failure.'

The fact that it did fail, and that Protestantism found itself uniquely vulnerable to secularization, is an illustration of the danger of trying to avoid the theological tensions referred to at the end of the last chapter.

In the new edition of T. S. Eliot's *The Idea of a Christian Society* there is an interesting review of the book by Maurice Reckitt, with Eliot's reply.[14] Reckitt accuses Eliot of envisaging a society in which 'the *religious* life of the people would be *largely* a matter of behaviour and conformity', a second-class Christianity, in other words, for the masses, with a fuller Christian witness being maintained by a more articulate and committed minority. He robustly rejects this as incompatible with the Gospel. Eliot's reply is pragmatic.

There is a fundamental dilemma from which it is no more possible for Mr Reckitt to escape than for me. If you design your Christian society only according to what your experience of human beings, and the history of the last nineteen hundred years, tells you is possible, then it must remain open to the charge of being sub-Christian. If you design it beyond experience and history, you are committed to utopian plans the impractibility of which will expose you to relapse into a Lutheran despair of this world.

He emphasizes that he was intending to express a minimal requirement for a society to be called Christian, not a goal to be aimed at by the Church. But the very idea that there can be minimal and maximal forms of allegiance sits uncomfortably within Protestant thought.

Catholicism has on the whole been able to cope better with the maintenance of high standards on the one hand, and a pragmatic recognition on the other hand that the faith of the masses is likely to operate at a lower level. There are signs of change, however, of a sacramentalism which is becoming exclusive rather than inclusive, and a more Protestant emphasis on interior meaning, stemming in

14   1982 edition, p. 114 seq.

part from the Second Vatican Council. Mary Douglas's remarks on the Bog Irish are instructive in this respect.[15]

The Bog Irish, she says, are primitive ritualists. Religion revolves around such simple and clear commitments as Friday abstinence. For an Irish girl, uprooted from home and living in a hostile environment, obedience to a simple rule is no empty symbol. It is a permanent reminder of where she belongs, and the fact that it enters once a week into her kitchen gives it an added significance. In this respect it is exactly parallel with kosher meat and Sabbath observance for the Jews.

But what has happened? Recognizing with modern charitable instincts the difficulties experienced by many Roman Catholics in actually keeping the fast, and stressing the value of interior intention over mere external observance, the English hierarchy, following a Papal ruling, 'decided that the best way of carrying out our Lord's command to do penance is for each of us to choose our own way of self-denial each Friday . . .'.

Now Roman Catholics can be like anybody else. And the displaced Irish girl has lost one of the markers, however tenuous, which enabled her to know her place in a cosmic scheme of salvation. Interiorizing a symbol, which in practice does its work as part of a larger social and cultural environment, trying to enter too self-consciously into its 'meaning', can effectively destroy it.

Not all operate on the simple level of Douglas's Bog Irish, but it would not be hard to tell similar stories of many who look to the Church of England for markers and guideposts as, perhaps distant, reminders of what they want to be, and find themselves offered something too intellectualized and too spiritualized to be of help to them.

Alan Wilkinson's book, already mentioned, is full of shattering evidence of the Church's 'failure to grasp the significance of inarticulate religion outside the church'.[16] Inarticulateness was confused with lack of faith, and for the most part chaplains failed to use the actual moments of religious awareness of those at the front. The soldiers lingered around 'the uncrossed threshold of religion . . . . The results of all the religious education were strangely small. The Church's teaching had come over as externalized dogma; only

15   Douglas, *Natural Symbols*, p. 59 seq.
16   Wilkinson, pp. 89, 118, 162, 238.

hymns lasted and gave delight.' In summing up his experience, one of the most perceptive chaplains, Oswin Creighton, wrote:

> The war reveals that the Englishman is the best hearted, most enduring, most ignorant and least original man in the world. The work of the church is to help him build up what he has not got on the basis of what he has. An understanding church is our great need.

When these words were written it was still perhaps possible to think in terms of a church which could build on the residues of inarticulate religion, and gradually aim to incorporate once more the whole nation. Today it is not. The submerged part of the iceberg is likely to remain submerged. More conscious of pluralism, we are more likely to accept that religious belief will remain confused, variegated, differing greatly in intensity and in external expression, and for the most part non-intellectual. The practical question facing the churches, and especially the established churches, is how far they are willing to acknowledge this confusion, and live with it, and try to understand it, and go on providing significant markers and linkages and means of access for those who discover their need of a more explicit and articulate faith.

For this to happen the churches themselves need a sufficiently strong base from which to operate. Without a committed membership and without definite beliefs a church ceases to act as a marker to those outside it. Nor can it maintain itself without evangelism, nor remain true to its own belief without generating a sense of mission. A church which goes too far in the direction of openness to the world, which simply and solely thinks of itself as the tip of an iceberg and draws no distinctions, is in danger of losing its identity. This is what was happening to the Roman Catholic Church in the Netherlands in the heyday of its liberalization.[17] It remains a perpetual temptation for the Church of England, a temptation to some extent mitigated in recent years by, of all things, financial pressures.

One of the results of the financial revolution of the seventies, which has forced Church of England parishes to become much more dependent on regular financial support from parishioners, has been to make an increase in congregational commitment imperative for

17   Martin, *A General Theory of Secularization*, p. 193.

survival. This has probably done more to change the character of the Church of England, and to push it in the direction of becoming a denomination with gathered congregations, just like other denominations, than any other single factor. In addition, the decrease in the number of clergy has imposed severe limitations on their work, forced them to spend more time in attending to the needs of their congregations and in dealing with specifically ecclesiastical matters, and has thus further reduced both the inclination and the opportunity to respond to the huge demands of uncommitted folk religionists.

Parishes, and parish clergy in particular, find themselves facing a very real dilemma. By concentrating on the committed, and by raising the barriers against nominal allegiance, they effectively unchurch large numbers of people who still think of themselves, in Eliot's sense, as part of a Christian society. Congregations which adopt exclusive policies have to weigh up the likely consequences for the broad social life of the area, and for individuals who discover that links with what they regard as 'their church' have been severed. Such congregations also have to face the risks involved in narrowing their own bases. In the Introduction mention was made of the study *Churches and Churchgoers*,[18] with its surprising conclusion that, statistically speaking, the strength of church membership is affected more by external social factors than by internal policies. It was suggested that the success of evangelism is closely related to the size of the pool of 'adherents' who move in and out of more committed membership. If this is true, then even on purely utilitarian grounds it would not seem a very sensible policy deliberately to empty the pool.

On the other hand, it is frequently said that overmuch attention to the needs of the uncommitted, dilutes the significance of church membership to the point at which it ceases to count for anything. It is when sacrifices are demanded, when membership costs something, that it begins to be worth having. And it is the exclusive churches, with a clear and simple gospel and high standards of commitment, which flourish. On the latter point it needs to be asked how far exclusivist policies actually enable churches to break into new markets for their members, or how far they are in practice as dependent on the pool of 'adherents' as any other churches. I

18   See page 7.

suspect that for the most part they pick up dissatisfied members of other churches, but have no evidence to prove it. The main point, however, stands firm, namely that exclusivist policies have real strengths, and that even those with the most liberal attitudes towards church membership have to draw the line somewhere. The lower reaches of the religious iceberg may well contain all sorts of nastiness whose religious dimension may be acknowledged, but whose manifestations must be totally rejected. As pointed out earlier, there are 'other gods', and nothing said about responding positively to folk religion must be allowed to obscure that fact.

But if lines have to be drawn somewhere, the question remains, where are they to be drawn? And how?

I want to suggest that the 'where?' depends on the 'how?' In a pluralist society Christian commitment has to be a matter of deliberate choice. It is in the choosing that Christian identity is affirmed. This is as true of Christian groups as it is of individuals. A group, therefore, which chooses as part of its Christian commitment to accept a measure of responsibility for those it sees as being outside itself, has a possible means of retaining its own sense of identity, and of avoiding the perils of exclusiveness. The choice itself is a sign of commitment. The responsibility chosen is a sign of openness. Both values can be affirmed.

The responsibility deliberately chosen and accepted is not just to be thought of as an evangelistic one, though it will almost certainly include that dimension. At its heart is an acknowledgement that God's kingdom transcends any actual expression of it in the church, that God works in individuals and in societies in ways which may not be immediately obvious, and that the special task of the church is to make explicit what God is doing, not to be the sole agent of it.

To choose to be involved in the life of the world, to care for people, to welcome even very inadequate expressions of faith, is in itself to make a huge act of faith in the reality of God's presence. This is what makes it possible to hold on to both sides of the dilemma. A church which sees its responsibility in these terms, and chooses to accept it, is not in danger of falling into indifferentism, nor is it likely to lack opportunities for costly service. It is essential, though, that the choice should not just be made once, and then forgotten. It is only by constantly reaffirming it that the commitment and vision of the core group, essential to any actual congregation, can be retained. And it is this which distinguishes the policy I am now suggesting from the placid unthinking acceptance of folk religion as if it created no problems.

It does. The problem of Christian identity cannot be ducked. But neither can the fact that religion, including the Christian religion, is a much more complicated phenomenon than any simple distinction between believers and non-believers will allow. Those who by God's grace are brought to an explicit affirmation of faith within an explicit Christian community do not in my view deny that faith, but rather see more deeply into its implications, when they recognize that God's activity is not limited to themselves. A church which deliberately chooses an open policy, which welcomes those whose beliefs may seem inadequate, without patronizing them, and which is not offended by those who seem merely to want to use it for their own convenience, is not thereby saying that its beliefs do not matter. It is signalling what David Jenkins in another context has called 'the impossibility and the necessity of the Church';[19] necessity, because without it there would be no Gospel; impossibility, because no actual church can represent that Gospel in its fulness, still less God in his transcendence.

If an open policy towards folk religion has to be continually reaffirmed in order to safeguard itself against complacency, then the question of where to draw the line can never be answered once-for-all. It is the constant wrestling with very practical and seemingly trivial problems like how to relate Remembrance Day or Mothering Sunday services more effectively both to the needs and expectations of those attending them, and to the insights of the Gospel, which will set its own limits.[20] The same is true of baptism policies. There is no one policy appropriate at all times and in all circumstances. The essential thing, as I see it, is to hear and respond to the needs actually being expressed, and to try to make them points of access to a fuller and more explicit Christian experience, without being too disappointed if the opportunities are refused. The line between sharing faith and prostituting it, draws itself in a church which cares without fussing, and witnesses without claiming exclusive possession of its truth.

19 The title of a paper in *Crucible* (July–September 1974) p. 108.
20 See Malcolm Grundy, 'The Death of Secular Man' in *Theology* (1979) LXXXII, pp. 349–54.

The key to such a policy is the choice to live responsibly in the world. And it is in this context that the issue of establishment, which has obvious links with folk religion, is best tackled.

6

Establishment

Established churches on the whole receive a bad press in sociological writings. Words like 'anachronism' and 'marginality' abound. Such churches are accused of clinging to a meaningless facade of social importance, whose substance has long since disappeared. Worse still, establishment is seen as encouraging active collusion with the social order. Establishment-minded churchmen, we are told, enjoy the appearance of success, a success bought at the cost of merely reflecting the social values of their day. It would be better to face facts, undo the remaining links between church and state, and let established churches find their freedom as one denomination among others.

Martin has a more sympathetic treatment of the subject than most,[1] and can serve usefully to link this theme with the dilemma facing clergy and parishes referred to at the end of the last chapter. He makes the point that even apart from any formal relationship between church and state, there is a pull towards collusion between religious and social values, a pull initially represented in the high social status enjoyed by clergy, whether they belong to an established church or not. The more clergy are felt to matter as part of the social scene, the more the values they are seen to represent, and the values of society itself, will be regarded as fundamentally in harmony.

But when things start to change, when churches are reduced to the status of voluntary organizations with a shrinking base in a secular, pluralist society, the clergy have to choose much more consciously what their role will be. Some internalize it, emphasize its 'religious' aspects to the exclusion of all others, and look for fulfilment in ritual activities, close-knit groups, charismatic

1 Martin, *A General Theory of Secularization*, pp. 278 seq.

93

phenomena, and direct aggressive evangelism. Others secularize their role, concentrating on limited therapeutic work, and becoming in effect quasi-social workers. Others try to maintain a role based on folk religion and civic piety, but become troubled by the extent to which this seems to imply social passivity, and to obscure other, sharper functions. Yet a fourth group to all intents and purposes step outside the structures, to adopt a general role as social prophets, while at the same time using their status within the structures to ram home criticism of the society which validates that status.

These are, of course, caricatures. Actual responses may combine all four elements. But the analysis may help to put the more limited issue of formal establishment in a broader context. There is no simple answer to questions about how a church should best relate to the society in which it is set. The various roles available to clergy illustrate the choices facing the churches themselves, and all have their disadvantages and limitations. The world of groups and liturgical observances can be suffocatingly small. Social repair work can provide an escape route from the ambiguities and uncertainties of explicit religion. Civic religion can be a threat to religious integrity. And free-wheeling prophecy can become self-indulgent and unreal.

The different approaches can correct and supplement one another, which is why it is as well to be cautious of disposing of any one of them. Nor must it be imagined that a disestablished church would find the act of disestablishment releasing it from social pressures which in fact impinge on all the churches, established and free. The realistic question for the Church of England is not, is there some ideal alternative to establishment? but what is the balance of advantage and disadvantage in remaining established?

First, though, it is important to dispose of a frequent source of confusion. The word 'establishment' is currently used in two quite distinct senses. There is a limited, technical, meaning, as when a church is described as 'established', where the word signifies an official and more or less well-defined relationship between church and state. The actual legal content of this may be quite small, as in the case of the Church of England, but it may have many overtones derived from history and convention. There is also a broad, and comparatively modern, use of the word 'Establishment' to refer to a nexus of people in English society who operate as a kind of 'master class', top politicians and civil servants, leaders in the various professional worlds, including leading churchmen, the editor of *The Times*, members of famous clubs, the key people with a vested interest in society as it is, and who, it is supposed, confer together to 'fix things'. In this second sense Establishment is an omnibus term for the real or imagined elite at the centre of English society.

For the Church of England to be established in the first sense does not necessarily imply membership of the Establishment in the second sense. True, it provides a means of access to influential circles for a limited number of people who would otherwise be unlikely to count for much in public life. The more secular society becomes, the more tenuous this access and the less significant the influence. But except in this very restricted and residual sense the established church is not, and has not for more than a century, been an effective part of the Establishment, despite popular misconceptions to the contrary.

The same applies to the phrase 'establishment-mindedness', which may mean simply that churchmen take seriously the responsibilities of belonging to a national church, or may mean an attitude of subservience to the powers that be. The pejorative overtones of the second sense easily rub onto the first one, but this is guilt by association, not a necessary connection. In what follows, I shall be using the word 'establishment' entirely in its first and technical sense, and will hope to show that its actual connotations are very different from those usually fastened on it by its critics. In a single chapter of this length, it is not possible to enter into the historical arguments, nor even to spell out in any detail the legal content of establishment, nor to consider the forms of establishment in other countries.[2] My concern is with its practical significance in England here and now.

What are the objections to it?

(1) It is said to be unreal, to invite delusions of grandeur, and to be positively misleading in obscuring the true, and desperate, state of religion in England. Hensley Henson was making the same point fifty years ago, when the statistics of church attendance were a great deal more healthy than they are now.

2 All the necessary information can be found in the Chadwick Report, *Church and State* (1970).

Like a magnificent roof ravaged by the death-watch beetle, yet marking by its splendid appearance a fatal though unheeded weakness, our ancient national Establishment, stripped of meaning and void of power, still dominates us by its aspect of immemorial and unalterable authority. It is a noble facade without a building behind it . . . it is our plain duty to face the fact that, in the circumstances of our modern world, national establishment is for Christianity unwholesome and potentially destructive.[3]

Written in 1933, the last sentence carries unmistakable echoes of events in Germany – of which more later. But the first sentence, with its reference to power, is also interesting. In terms of power, grandeur, numerical significance, the Church of England had slipped far by 1933, and has slipped even further today. Much of what has been said in earlier chapters of this book contributes to the picture of a church which has lost most, if not all, of its former power in an increasingly fragmented social order. Henson's point can be conceded.

But is, or ought, establishment to be conceived primarily in terms of power and grandeur? No doubt it once was. The temptation to equate 'reality' with power is one of those delusions from which advocates of disestablishment want to deliver the church. I am not myself convinced that disestablishment is necessary for this task. The facts of life will do it by themselves. But suppose such deliverance from this particular temptation were to take place, what then? Might it be that the 'reality' of establishment, the 'reality' of which power-seeking is a distortion, would be discovered elsewhere?

For myself, and I suspect for a great many Church of England clergy and laity, the point of impact of establishment in parish, as well as in national life, is found, not in power-seeking, but in the impetus it gives to some of the perceptions described in the last chapter. As its critics have rightly seen, folk religion is one of the key issues. And in this context the reality of establishment expresses itself through a sense of responsibility for the nation as a whole, and in particular for those whose religion is mostly inarticulate and submerged.

To some this may be a further reason for rejecting it. There are

3   H. Hensley Henson, *Bishoprick Papers* (1946), p. 47. See also his *Disestablishment* (1929).

others, of whom Peter Cornwall is a notable example, who adopt an intermediate position.[4] They do not reject folk religion, nor the belief that churches should have a national role, nor do they wish to compromise traditional Anglican liberality. They just deny the dependence of such attitudes on the fact of establishment. Cornwall writes, 'Nothing in my experience of the Church of England so far leads me to believe that its liberality and openness depend upon its special legal status.'

In a narrow sense this is obviously true. Members of the Church of England are not constantly referring to its established status as a justification for their policies; indeed clergy who rely too readily on their status as 'parsons' and appeal too blatantly to their supposed rights and privileges, do much to discredit the idea. Nor would the whole ethos of the church undergo a sudden and drastic revolution if disestablishment were to take place. Other churches, besides the Church of England, have a lively social awareness, sometimes more lively, and the Anglican church overseas shares something of the same ethos. Yet I find it hard to believe that in the long run legal status makes no difference to the way in which a church thinks about itself, and I am not nearly as sanguine as Cornwall in thinking that the present tendencies in the Church of England towards denominationalism would not be reinforced by disestablishment.

As I see it the difference, such as it is, made by the fact of establishment, comes to light primarily in the instinctive reactions of Church of England members towards those who are not actively members of any particular church. For members of non-established churches there is always a prior question to be asked: What are my grounds for being concerned with this or that person? For members of an established church the sense of responsibility is instinctive and natural. I say this not in any way in criticism of other churches. Having been a member of a non-established church in Scotland, I know from personal experience how circumstances shape one's spontaneous responses. And I can also witness to a certain amount of non-conformist anger and frustration at the arrogance of estab-

4   This chapter has been written before the publication of Peter Cornwall's *The Church And the Nation: The Case for Disestablishment* (1983). In what follows I rely on his earlier note of dissent in the Chadwick Report, pp. 79–82.

lished churchmen who make claims for themselves of the kind spelt out in this paragraph.

But facts are facts, and it seems to me that even this anger witnesses to the fact of a real instinctive difference. To be conscious of belonging to a national church is to be given a broad sense of responsibility for all and sundry. The motive for exercising that responsibility may, and should, be rooted in the Gospel, but the way it is perceived cannot help being affected by the context. And it is not just feelings of responsibility which make a difference. It is the knowledge that one is on the receiving end of perceptions that one *ought* to be responsible. People have expectations of an established church which they would not have if it were not established. Whether these are helpful or unhelpful, good or bad, is not for the moment the point at issue. The fact is that they exist.

This shared admission of responsibility, though in many cases it may be minimal in extent and virtually impossible to fulfil, is a major part of the continuing 'reality' of establishment. The fact that it is a legal responsibility, openly acknowledged by both church and nation, reinforces the perceptions which underlie it and which would probably not survive in the long run without this public backing.

(2) A corollary to the claim that establishment is unreal and invites delusions of grandeur, is the charge that it smacks inescapably of privilege. The fact that it is easy to treat it in ways which raise nonconformist hackles has already been mentioned. But it is the whole style of a church in which bishops hobnob with Top People, in which Christian involvement in politics is thought to be satisfied by an episcopal presence in the House of Lords, and which gives the appearance of being important even if the substance is lacking, that gives offence. What have ancient privileges and worldly honours to do with serving a crucified Lord? And what can a church which seems to exude an air of effortless superiority say to the poor, the powerless and the underprivileged?

There has been much writing on this theme in recent years,[5] both from a national and an international perspective. In a recent Church of England consultation with overseas assessors the issue of establishment, which at first caused puzzlement and misunderstanding

5   e.g. David Sheppard's *Bias to the Poor* (1983), and many W.C.C. documents, including the report of the Melbourne conference. Martin Conway's *Through the Eyes of the Poor* (1980) makes the point sharply.

among the visitors from other churches, was ultimately refined down to this single issue of the church's privileged style.[6] The criticism is a serious one and I do not pretend there is any easy answer without some radical changes in the way establishment is understood. A clearer separation between establishment and 'the Establishment' might be a first step in this.

But there is another side of the picture, expressed very powerfully by Daniel Jenkins, and all the more striking in that it comes from a Welsh dissenter. He castigates the Church of England for trying 'to sidle quietly out of the responsibilities of establishment', of being 'more interested in herself as an institution than she is in England',[7] and 'failing to think imaginatively enough about the future of England in the light of the Christian faith'. He laments her relative failure to minister appropriately to those who carry enormous responsibilities, many of whom 'are hard pressed to find someone independent and trustworthy to whom they can talk about their personal and public problems. The Church of England would appear to be quite magnificently equipped to provide the help which they need.' He doubts whether disestablishment would give her freedom to minister to the nation in new ways.

The present arrangement limits that freedom only marginally. What would be much more likely is that large areas of her life would fade into the amiable and nostalgic dimness of a body like the Church of Ireland in our time. But that would not be the whole story, for the Church of England has been too much involved for that to happen over the whole of her life. What would also happen would be that the things which the Church of England has done well in the past will no longer be done, with grave social consequences. If she gives up trying to help those in authority avoid the corrupting influence of power, and contents herself with being the domestic chaplain of those who once held power, along with their retainers, she and they will decline into a querulous and lonely old age while those in real power go their own way.[8]

He goes on:

6   *To a Rebellious House?* (1981) C.I.O. Report.
7   Jenkins, *The British*, p. 68–9.
8   ibid., p. 94.

99

She may miss many of the opportunities of effective influence which are open to her in the common life of England and of Britain as a whole unless she resists her present tendency to regard being established as a burden to be shrugged off rather than an inescapeable responsibility which she has inherited, and which has been a major factor in making her what she is.

Talk of privileges, in other words, misses the point. Mere privilege is to be deplored. But privilege which comes as the other side of the coin of responsibility can only be avoided by shirking the responsibility. Let me illustrate the point with reference to bishops in the House of Lords.

To those who do not know it from within, the House of Lords can seem the haunt of privilege *par excellence*. But when one tries to spell out in concrete terms what the actual privileges are, they do not seem nearly so impressive. A place to hang one's coat and park one's car and eat a reasonably cheap lunch in central London; an expense allowance which just, only just, covers costs; access to a library and parliamentary papers; contact with interesting people; a public platform. The rest is sheer hard work. It is, of course, a privilege to be able to play a part in the processes of government, but when one is actually engaged in it the responsibilities, the hours spent in reading papers, preparing speeches and listening to the interminable speeches of others, loom much larger. The so-called privileges are simply the necessary conditions for doing the job.

But, says the critic, it is not these things which are summed up in the word 'privilege'. It is the fact of bishops being there at all. Indeed, it is the fact that the House of Lords is there at all. Why not be satisfied with lay Christians doing a lay job, and winning their right to do so by being elected?

These are large questions which deserve much more than the paragraph or two I can give them. Both Houses of Parliament, of course, contain many lay Christians of all denominations who do not hide their Christianity. The bishops are not, and do not pretend to be, the only Christian spokesman. They do, however, constitute a visible and permanent reminder of the relationship between Church and State. The fact that they are not peers in the ordinary sense but form part of a distinct section of the House, the Lords Spiritual, the fact that they sit on separate benches and, unlike other peers, wear robes when attending debates, emphasize the point that it is their presence *as bishops* which is significant. Many bishops have in the past, and still do, make a valuable contribution as individuals to the work of the House. But in a field of activity which is rich in symbolism of many kinds, it is the symbolism rather than individual success or corporate power, which is important and which still manages to represent a residual national commitment to the Christian faith.

Whether this national commitment is a good thing or a bad thing is, of course, one of the recurring themes of this book. The point being argued at present is that, if it is a good thing, then the presence of bishops in the House of Lords is an appropriate symbol of it, and that it is not adequate to argue in reply that there are plenty of other Christians there already.

But is is a good thing? The classic defence of establishment, from the point of view of the good of the nation, was made in a speech in the House of Lords by Cosmo Lang in 1913 on the subject of the church in Wales. He asked

> Whether in the public corporate life of the nation there is to be any assertion at all of its religious basis, of its acknowledgement of Almighty God, of its concern with the religious life of the people . . . To some of us [the State] is something which we do not as individuals compose but which as individuals we enter, and which from the very first, by virtue of its own intrinsic character, moulds and frames our life and being. It has an organic unity and spirit of its own, and that character and spirit are built up by tradition and associations running far back into the past. Its life is expressed not only by the policies and pursuits of the present, but also by a sort of subconscious continuity which endures and profoundly affects the character of each generation of citizens who enter within it. The question before us, as some of us consider it, is whether just there, in that inward region of the national life where anything that can be called its unity and character is expressed, there is or is not to be this witness to some ultimate sanction to which the nation looks, some ultimate ideal which it professes. It is in our judgement a very serious thing for a state to take out of that corporate heart of its life any acknowledgement at all of its concern with religion.[9]

9   Cited in Norman, *Church and Society in England*, p. 278.

This is a powerful argument, weakened but not destroyed by the growth of pluralism since Lang's day. It has been suggested already in chapter 2 that it is precisely continuities of this kind which render pluralism stable. Ancient institutions have to change. The House of Lords has to change, though the chances of reaching agreement on how it should do so are not very high. But it is apparent over and over again from the disastrous consequences of well-meaning legislation, that the cutting of ancient links and the rationalizing of ancient assumptions and the legislating away of ancient safeguards, often destroys a great deal more than the legislators had in mind.

If the continuing relationship between Church and State means anything, then the peculiar forms in which it is expressed may change, as they have changed in the past, but they should not be tampered with lightly. In particular, the issue of privilege is not going to disappear. I shall be looking in chapter 9 at ways in which it might be made a less divisive issue as between the different churches in Britain. On the wider question of the way in which an established church *appears* to be privileged, and so cuts itself off from the mass of the people who resent privilege and feel themselves to be under-privileged, it is difficult to write from a privileged position. The dangers of self-deception are all too real. The criticisms have to be heard.

I sometimes wonder, however, how many of the innumerable critics who seize on such obvious signs of so-called privilege as the fact that a few bishops still live in medieval castles, have ever paused to do more than indulge in reflex reactions. The issues are not those of luxury and extravagance, as those who bear the burdens of living in such structures will testify. Nor are they properly to do with 'the image' of a bishop. A bishop who lives in a wealthy suburb in a prime example of stockbroker's Tudor is much more effectively 'typed' as belonging to a particular social setting, than one whose provenance is undeniably historical and ecclesiastical. The main issue, as I see it, is not unlike the issues which arise over the preservation of ancient parish churches. A particular building may have become absurdly pretentious in the light of the needs of those who actually use it. Yet to dispose of it might sever all kinds of emotional and historical links which our increasingly rootless society can ill afford to lose. To discuss such matters simply in terms of 'privileges' and 'images' is to miss the point.

In the end, for me, it is Jenkins' warning about running away from responsibilities which strikes home hardest. He also has interesting suggestions about a more mature ecumenism in which different churches would carry different responsibilities on behalf of one another, without all seeking to do the same thing. In some such way it might be possible to shift the emphasis to where it belongs, namely towards the different kinds of tasks which need to be performed by the whole Christian community, in all its diversity, in relation to the whole life of the nation. Within such a broad-based approach the particular issue of privilege might fade into a proper insignificance.

(3) A third major objection to establishment centres on the spiritual freedom of the church. A fashionable way of expressing it is to ask whether an established church can be prophetic. I must confess to some doubts about the modern use of the word 'prophetic' as applied to churches, and still more as applied indiscriminately to clergymen. Gill[10] has argued recently that only individuals can be prophets, and that there are inherent contradictions in a church as a whole, or those whose role within it is primarily priestly, trying to claim gifts which belong properly within a different context. The prophet is inevitably something of an outsider, 'a troubler of Israel',[11] and the point at issue is not whether 'all the Lord's people' are prophets, but whether they are prepared to hear those whom he sends. Clerical guilt at not having 'a prophetic ministry' is unnecessary and misplaced. But does an established church encourage prophecy, and does it have the freedom, and is it likely to be willing, to respond when prophets in its midst have made its duty clear?

The question about freedom is answered relatively easily. There are nowadays very few restrictions on the freedom of the Church of England to do what it decides is right. Parliamentary control of legislation operates within strict limits and is almost wholly concerned with the protection of the rights of citizens in what is appropriately regarded as 'their' church. On the rare occasions when there are tensions between Church and Parliament, the key issue is always whether a relatively small elected body of church activists is competent to speak for the inarticulate religious life of the nation. We shall return to this point in the next chapter.

10   R. Gill, *Prophecy and Praxis* (1981).
11   1 Kings 18:17.

Outside the Parliamentary context, the main residual symbol of state control and the main bone of contention is, of course, the method of appointing bishops. A great deal has been said in the last year or so in criticism of the power retained by the Prime Minister in making the final choice. I would be more impressed by these criticisms, insofar as they relate to particular instances, if there had been the slightest indication from the church body responsible, the Crown Appointments Commission, that this power had been, or was likely to be, abused. As it is, the only people who know how the system works at first hand, seem satisfied with it. I do not see, therefore, that there are any pragmatic grounds for alarm.

But what about the principle? How can a church claim to be free when its chief officers are appointed by somebody who need not even belong to it? Put like that, the implied criticism in the question is hard to counter. But the question is itself highly misleading. It ignores the subtlety of the procedures and the safeguards built into them. Nobody can become a bishop unless the church, through its Archbishops, is willing to consecrate him. To veto a particular appointment by a refusal to consecrate might be costly in terms of Church/State relationships, but it remains a perpetual possibility, and hence an ultimate guarantee of freedom.

The question also overlooks the very restricted nature of the choice available to a Prime Minister. The restrictions lie, not only in the procedures themselves, but in the size of the constituency from which appropriate appointments might be made. It is not hard for the Appointments Commission to have ample evidence about all conceivable candidates.

More fundamentally the question sidesteps one of the major implications of being a national church, namely that bishops are expected to be more than diocesan pastors, but have an inescapable national role. Dunstan makes the point succinctly:

Are bishops and deans still to be men of such stature, and their offices still of such significance, that they count for something in the national life? that it matters who shall occupy these positions? If so, the Crown is the apt embodiment of the national interest.[12]

12 From Mark Santer (ed.), *Their Lord and Ours* (1982) in an essay entitled *Corporate Union and Body Politic*, p. 144.

The precise way in which this national interest should be represented is a subject for continuing debate, and the present system is certainly not the only possible one. But to make the appointment of bishops wholly a matter for the more active members of the visible church community, would be to make a theological choice about the nature of the church, which would in the long run be incompatible with establishment, and could well be restrictive rather than liberating. Rome has its own way of counterbalancing local ecclesiastical enthusiasms, but this is not a way at present open to the Church of England.

The formal freedom of the Church of England is not, as I see it, seriously compromised by the fact of establishment. In fact rather the reverse. The embodiment of many rights and privileges in the law of the land gives individual members of the Church of England a degree of freedom which they might not otherwise enjoy. This is not the kind of freedom which leaders and administrators especially welcome, but it is important that individual freedom should be given due weight in relation to corporate freedom, particularly in the light of the issues discussed in the last chapter.

Whether, apart from these formal freedoms, establishment makes the Church of England less willing to encourage, listen, and respond to the voice of prophecy, is a different question altogether, and one to which it is much less easy to give a confident answer. The reasons for this are worth exploring. They relate closely to the theme of responsibility which has been running through this chapter.

A church which includes within its activities a ministry towards those with secular power, whether at national or local level, is bound to react differently from one whose 'prophecy' is delivered from a distance. This can look like subservience. 'Power corrupts', says the critic. And if it does not actually corrupt, at least it generates caution, the fear of losing favour and privileges. There is an uncomfortable element of truth in such accusations.

But there is more truth, at least within my own experience, in the perception that the key difference made by proximity to secular power is not one of attitude, but one of knowledge. To be close to those in power is to have some first-hand knowledge of the complexity of the actual choices facing them. This has a devastating effect on prophetic certainties. And actually to share responsibility is even more devastating. It is trite but true that it is easier to solve the world's problems in the comfort of a distant armchair than to decide in minute particulars what actually needs to be done.

As I see it, the world of the powerful – and I am thinking of politicians in particular – needs two kinds of help from a church responsive to the voice of prophecy. They need help in holding onto some distant simple vision; and they need help in actually facing the conflicts and contradictions on the road.

Simplicity is easier to talk about than to achieve. It comes, not from shirking thought, but from thinking things *through*. Above all it comes from having roots in basic truths and values which are not in danger of being undermined by the confusions of actual experience. There has to be a tough simple centre to Christian conviction. There is also a simplicity which comes from looking at complex problems from a radically different viewpoint. A church which genuinely provides a voice for the inarticulate and can remind the powerful, out of its own experience, of how things look from the other end of the scale, has a basis for stating some simple home truths.

Such simple, radical perceptions are necessary. It is not for nothing that much of politics runs on slogans. There is an honourable place for the constant repetition of simple moral judgements. Over-simplifications may be a bad basis for practical policies, but they can have the effect of waking up the complacent and changing unthinking habits. Much of what seems superficial and unreal in political life stems from the need felt by politicians to protect themselves from debilitating uncertainty by various means designed to simplify the issues and boost their own self-confidence. It would be unfair to grudge them this. There is a limit to the amount of self-knowledge and self-questioning which it is reasonable to expect in those who bear huge responsibilities.

But these simplicities belong ultimately to the distant vision. On the road itself they are not enough. Neither is it enough for churches to go on repeating great moral platitudes on such matters as peace and justice and human dignity, nor to try to lift every problem out of its context to view it *sub speci aeternitatis*. There has to be some resource and encouragement for meeting complexity head-on here and now, for bearing the strain of uncertainty, for living with paradox, for surviving failure. There is a prophetic ministry in demonstrating to people that things are not quite as simple as they thought they were, which is just as important as the prophetic ministry of the grand simple vision. I have tried to demonstrate in a previous book[13] that the Christian faith has unique resources for handling this kind of complexity, and will not elaborate the point further.

The key question is what this analysis tells us about establishment. Is an established church likely to lose its spiritual freedom and insight through proximity to the sources of power? If I am right, there is more danger that it may lose the simple vision, than fail to respond to complexity. Its ministry can therefore become lop-sided, and this is a real weakness; but it is not necessarily an argument for disestablishment. It would seem to me rather an argument for maintaining close links with dissenting traditions of various kinds in which the capacity for simple vision is sharper. This is what already happens to some extent within the British Council of Churches, and it is no accident that its social pronouncements are usually a good deal more radical than those of the Church of England. It is significant, though, for the argument which will follow, that some of the spiritual freedom of the Church of England is thus seen to be entailed in the freedom of bodies outside it.

(4) The fourth objection to establishment follows from this and can be dealt with much more briefly. It is a two-pronged argument from ecumenism. It is argued, first, that establishment is a hindrance to ecumenism, in that non-established churches would not be prepared to accept its conditions in the event of full organic union. The second prong is that ecumenism has made establishment unnecessary in that the former national responsibilities of the Church of England are now more properly exercised by ecumenical bodies like the British Council of Churches.

In the somewhat bleak ecumenical climate following the rejection of the Covenanting proposals, the arguments may seem less strong than they were, but they remain important, particularly the latter. My full response to them will have to wait until chapter 9, but I have already sketched out a preliminary answer on page 103, following some hints from Daniel Jenkins. In any conceivable ecumenism of the future there is likely to be a great deal of diversity. This is not only because churches do actually differ, but because they need each other's differences to make up their own deficiencies. The differences can be made to complement one another. I see no

13   John Habgood, *A Working Faith* (1980).

reason, therefore, why within this kind of diversity one church, or section of a united church, should not accept particular responsibilities formerly associated with establishment, and regard them as a service performed by that church on behalf of the others. In just the same way another church, or section of the church, would continue to represent the necessary element of dissent.

The key to such a division of function within a wider ecumenism would be the understanding of establishment first and foremost in terms of responsibility, which has been the main theme of this chapter. How practicable it would be for this responsibility to be extended to other churches or transferred, say, to the British Council of Churches or whatever grows out of it, and how acceptable this would be to the churches concerned, remains to be seen. I incline to the view that establishment is a burden which not all will want to share, indeed should not share, if they want to retain their distinctive contributions within the life of the whole. But that *some* church should bear it is important.

The little remaining privileges which belong to the aura of establishment, the salutations in the market place and the seat at top table at feasts, are already for the most part shared much more widely than they used to be. I suspect that the limits to such sharing will in the end be set by the limits of the dissenting conscience. It is much easier for episcopal churches which have a high doctrine of the symbolic role of clergy to live with this aura, than churches which deliberately play down differences of status.

The point can be illustrated by the sad failure to appoint more than two non-Anglican clergy, specifically as clergy, to the House of Lords. Lord Soper and Lord Macleod are both distinguished individuals who have given great service to the House, but there is no way in which they can be seen as representing their churches. Nor would their churches tolerate it if they did. Ideas about 'extending the establishment', therefore, run into difficulties which are likely to be just as intractable ecclesiastically as they might be constitutionally.

It remains true that the churches working together can do a great deal more for the life of the nation than the Church of England could ever achieve by itself; and the same is probably true of Scotland. Some sort of *de facto* ecumenical 'establishment' seems not only possible but desirable. But this is not likely to be achieved by the established churches running away from the *de jure* responsibilities they already possess.

So far in this chapter I have examined the four major objections commonly made to the establishment of the Church of England. I have conceded that there are some strong arguments, and that the character of its establishment has changed and needs to change still further. There are no absolutes in these matters. It is a question of making a particular judgement at a particular time and place. In my present judgement the overall case for disestablishment, now or in the foreseeable future, is not convincing.

One almost inevitable consequence of disestablishment would be the alienation of large numbers of people whose residual allegiance to the Church of England is bound up with the perception that in some obscure way it represents 'England'. The allegiance of many such people is already under severe strain. Religious purists would like to see them go, and would welcome disestablishment for precisely that reason. I myself believe that their departure would be a tragic loss, for them, for the church and for the nation. There, in a nutshell, is the heart of the choice.

At the beginning of chapter 2 brief reference was made to the possible effect of disestablishment on the Crown. The link between the Monarchy, the sense of national identity, and the persistence of a national commitment, however tenuous, to one kind of religion and morality in preference to others, needs much more careful exploration than can be given it here. In particular it would be interesting to know what effect, if any, the Queen's relationship to the Churches of England and Scotland has on the way she is perceived in these nations, and whether this differs from perceptions in Commonwealth countries without established churches. It might be discovered, for example, that something of the religious dimension of her office in Britain carries over into these other contexts. Manifestly it does so in her own person, but there might be more to it than that.

In fact it is difficult to know what a purely secular monarchy would look like. The mystique of the Crown has irreducibly religious roots, and at the very least secularization would result in a drastic loss of symbolic overtones. It would also remove a unique point of contact between secular and religious authority. There are reasons to be cautious, therefore, about supposing that disestablishment would leave the Monarchy untouched.

A second reason for caution about unsuspected losses through disestablishment is not perhaps highly relevant at present except on odd occasions, but might become so if nationalistic feelings and 'little Englandism' were to increase. Much of this book so far, and this chapter in particular, has concentrated on national life, national needs, national identity and so on. But this is only part of the story, and a minor part of it at that. The huge implications of living in a shrinking world, of growing interdependence between nations, of global problems which can only be solved by much more international co-operation than the world has been accustomed to in the past, this whole urgently important dimension of modern existence has so far been deliberately relegated to the background.

But even if nations may try, foolishly, to live for themselves alone, no church can afford to do so. A Christianity which has lost its international vision has lost its hold on the Gospel. One of the constant tasks of a church, therefore, in relation to national life, is to keep on opening up this international dimension, to be supportive of the nation without being seduced by nationalism, to affirm national identity, while showing its dependence on a similar affirmation of the identity and well-being of others.

An established church, with a growing consciousness of its own international and ecumenical dimensions, is in a potentially strong position to give just this kind of witness, unwelcome though it may sometimes be. Only the Church of England could have insisted on counter-balancing the nationalistic thrust of the Falklands celebrations, precisely because of its relationship to the nation. And the fact that it did so was a direct consequence of its developing relationship with the Anglican Communion and other world Christian bodies. It may seem bizarre to value a national church as one of the antidotes to nationalism, but this is because a church which is true to itself can never *just* be the church of the nation.

A third reason for caution about disestablishment has been expressed on more than one occasion by Clifford Longley in articles in *The Times*. He has argued that divisions between Catholics and Protestants, conservatives and radicals, within the Church of England are so deep that it is in effect held together only by the fact of being established. A common concern about fulfilling a national role serves to paper over the cracks.

This is an exaggeration, as anyone who knows the Church of England from within must surely realize. It is in any case refuted by the fact that disestablishment is itself a divisive issue. But it can at least serve to pose an important question: How well would the Church of England survive the strain of disestablishment if it were to happen?

The answer must depend on the circumstances. If it were to be undertaken on the basis of general principle, because a party advocating disestablishment had gained a majority in the General Synod, then in my view it would be highly divisive and would almost certainly weaken the Church of England rather than strengthen it. If, on the other hand, disestablishment were to be forced on the Church by the State, because the Church had held firm on some principle judged to be central to its life, the chances are that it would strengthen and unite the Church.

The parallels with Germany and South Africa are instructive. Hinchliff asks himself why the churches of South Africa did not cut their links with the State after the Sharpeville massacres, along the lines of the Confessing Church in Germany after the rise of Hitler. He answers, very honestly, that in Germany the Church came under direct attack through the Nazi attempt to bring it under State control.

> This, fortuitously, made it easier for members of the confessing movement to give their action organizational form. The protest against the State quite naturally became a structured dissent, a quasi-denominational separation . . . with an organization, synodical meetings and formal leadership of its own.[14]

In Africa, by contrast, there was no overt pressure by the State on the organizational structure of the churches.

> To become a confessing church would have had to be a directly *political* action with none of the ambiguity of the confessing movement in Germany . . . Since the official structures and doctrines of the churches were not openly attacked, any constitution designed for a new 'Church' would have had to assert that opposition to *apartheid* was one of its fundamental principles and that would have seemed like a proclamation that a political opinion was of the *esse* of the church.

It is an obvious and simple rule that pressure from without unites,

14 Hinchliff, *Holiness and Politics*, pp. 106–7.

and pressure from within divides. But perhaps it is not a bad rule to follow on the issue of disestablishment. A church must maintain its integrity. It must do what it believes to be right, with due regard for the feelings of those for whom it is responsible. If the State were to decide that it no longer wished to be linked with a church of this kind, then so be it. The church would survive.

But if the church were to decide that it was over-burdened by establishment, or if it were to go searching for some imagined new freedom, or if it were to restrict itself deliberately to a small group of activists then, if the arguments of this chapter have any validity, disestablishment would be both a symptom of and a recipe for decline.

7

The Bureaucratic Church

'When everything about a people is for the time growing weak and ineffective,' wrote G. K. Chesterton, 'it begins to talk about efficiency . . . Vigorous organisms talk not about their processes, but about their aims. . .'.[1]

Like most Chestertonian paradoxes this is no more than a half-truth. But it strikes home, as many hard-pressed ordinary church members will testify. Churches in decline seem to multiply bureaucracies. The weaker the local base on which everything rests, the more pervasive and dominatingly efficient seems the central machinery.

There is a spiritual truth in his paradox, too. Kosuke Koyama writes charmingly and pointedly about the 'inefficiency' of God.[2] God moves at a human pace and on a human scale, as concerned with the ox-cart as with the supersonic air-liner. Writing in an almost totally different context, Rowan Williams[3] makes the interesting suggestion that there is a connection between the modern taste for violent fantasy entertainment, films about monsters, disasters and demons, and modern feelings of helplessness in face of a technological and bureaucratic juggernaut which seems to be out of control, and heading for war. Many others write about the dehumanization of modern consciousness. There is a huge theological theme waiting to be explored, about the relation between technological efficiency and human values.

But the immediate concern of this chapter is with church life, and the extent to which the churches themselves have been caught up in this process, and hence come to share some of the ills of the societies to which they belong. The pressures towards efficiency,

1   G. K. Chesterton. *Heretics* (1905), p. 17.
2   Kosuke Koyama, *Waterbuffalo Theology* (1974), ch. 5.
3   Rowan Williams, *The Truce of God* (1983), ch. 1.

bureaucratization, centralization are felt by all institutions in a modern society, simply because they are institutions, and regardless of their aims.

This happens even when churches go far along the road towards privatization. Berger puts it thus:

> [Voluntary associations] are meant to fill the gap left by the underinstitutionalization of the private sphere. There is, however, a built-in paradox in the way in which they function. If they retain the optional, and therefore artificial, quality of private life, they are not able to meet the demand for stability and reliability that brought them about in the first place. If, on the other hand, they are so constructed as to meet these demands, they increasingly take on the character of the larger institutions of modern society; they become bureaucratized, and therefore anonymous, abstract . . .
>
> The discontents engendered by the structures of modernity in the public sphere have a disconcerting way of reappearing in the private sphere.[4]

Growing institutions show the same symptoms as declining ones, but in declining ones they are more obvious, because there is less scope for healthy inefficiency and greater dependence on the centre. Hence Chesterton's paradox, and hence the frustration felt by many church members, who wonder why an increasing proportion of their income seems to go to the support of unproductive bureaucrats. Such feelings can be especially strong in the churches, since they of all bodies, it seems, ought to be so structured as to witness to a different set of values.

To put the whole problem in a larger sociological context is not to solve it; indeed it is doubtful whether in a society as complex as ours any solution is possible. But particular frustrations can lose some of their personal sting when seen in more general terms. This needs to be said, because some church people go so far as to think of the growth of church bureaucracy as a kind of conspiracy. The truth is that it has been an inevitable and necessary response to the changing patterns of society, and without it the churches could not have survived other than in isolated pockets. The realistic question is not, is there an alternative to bureaucracy? but how can a

4   Berger *et al.*, *The Homeless Mind*, p. 168.

bureaucratic system be so tempered as to serve the true aims of a church, rather than obscure them?

This is the question which Kenneth Thompson explored in his well-known study of organizational change in the Church of England leading up to the creation of the General Synod.[5] In particular he documented the struggle between two organizational patterns, backed by different systems of authority, which synodical government was supposed to bring together. On the one hand there is the rational, administrative and representative system of synods, boards and committees. On the other there is the traditional, pastoral, hierarchical system, staffed by the clergy, and finding its fullest expression in the – largely undefined – authority of bishops. These two have never been fully integrated, and probably ought not to be, for a good theological reason to which we shall return a little later.

Meanwhile, as Thompson shows, it is possible to see how even on the purely practical level, the untidiness has its advantages. A wholly rational church structure would not be as resilient in containing the tensions between different parties and interests and shades of belief, as the present complex system of checks and balances. In addition, the Church of England's refusal simply to think of itself as a denomination, has depended in large measure on the close relationship with secular society which its pastoral structure has traditionally given it.

Centralization and rationalization have loosened these links with secular society, and have been in danger of increasing some of the internal tensions. In an essay written after the first five years of synodical government, I pointed out how the new synodical structures have accelerated the process.

A more efficient and democratic system of government, and there is no doubt that in many respects the General Synod is both, tends to sharpen the consciousness of an institution. Issues which previously might have been debated in the decent obscurity of the Convocations, are now out in the open. Awareness of real power, though it is generally exercised with commendable sensitivity towards minority opinions, can give a sharpness to decision-making, which is a far cry from the bumbling image of the Church as it once was. This is not a lament for past ineffi-

5   Kenneth A. Thompson, *Bureaucracy and Church Reform* (1970).

ciency, but a straightforward assertion that a new form of government in itself produces deep changes in an institution, quite apart from what those in power actually decide to do. The thrust is in the direction of greater definition and self-consciousness.[6]

I went on to list some of the changes, all in the direction of making the Church of England a more centralized, exclusive and self-contained religious body, and suggested some remedies.

Before considering these, it is important to unpack a little further various meanings of the word 'bureaucracy' so as to see more clearly the different kinds of conflict, some fruitful others not so fruitful, which it engenders. Thompson lists four:[7]

(1) In essence bureaucracy is simply a particular form of organization, giving high value to rationality and efficiency. It tends towards a system of rational–legal control, in which authority is vested in representative bodies. When the word is used in this neutral, non-pejorative sense, the main problems it creates for churches are theological ones. As mentioned earlier, the long history of reform in the Church of England can be seen as a struggle between two different understandings of the church, two systems of control, two concepts of authority, the one rational and representative, the other traditional and hierarchical.

Insofar as churches are institutions like any others, then rational and representative forms of organization are entirely appropriate to them. But is this all that churches are? It is precisely because this claim is denied that other kinds of structure are seen to have a vital role. Churches, we are told, are not democracies, and should not try to be. They live 'under the gospel'. Their ultimate authority is the authority of God. Their life is a response to what God has given them, and this 'givenness' requires structural expression.

Other institutions may claim that they too live 'under' some body of knowledge or expertize which gives them their distinctive characteristics. If Christianity is conceived as being no more than a message, the comparison is a fair one, and the distinctiveness of church structure loses its point. But for those who wish to stress that the message is somehow embodied, that the existence of the

6 John Habgood, 'Directions for the Church of England' in *Theology* LXXIX (1976), p. 132.
7 Thompson, p. 220 seq.

Church as 'a people' is an essential feature of the message itself, the need for some special structural expression of the fact is paramount. This is the key role played by the traditional hierarchical structure.

The parallel existence of two types of structure, therefore, the rational and the hierarchical, is not just the end-product of a series of political compromises. It is a valid expression of the nature of the church itself, an institution but claiming to be more than an institution. This is the crucial theological point.

Other advantages in the dual system stem from this, and some have already been mentioned. When they are in proper balance, each system should be able to compensate for the major operational deficiencies of the other – the potential impersonality of bureaucracy and the potential authoritarianism of hierarchy.

(2) A second common meaning of 'bureaucracy' underlines its pathological features. It is seen as a kind of ecclesiastical encephalitis, obstructing effective operation. There are the familiar complaints of red tape, endless meetings, delays and referrals. There is also the fear of constant growth, endless refinement of procedures, endless elaboration of structures.

The fears are certainly not groundless, even in times of stringency when the actual number of administrators may be declining. Rules can multiply without any corresponding increase in the number of those who have to apply them. There is a nice illustration of legislative encephalitis in the steady growth in the size and complexity of the Standing Orders of the Church of England's General Synod. These now occupy a closely printed book of 120 pages, and grow at the rate of two or three pages a year. Methodists could doubtless tell the same tale.

A major disadvantage of this perception of bureaucracy, as of those which follow, is that it encourages the two control systems to work against each other. Thompson notes how clergy resistance to bureaucratic growth and elaboration can create a crippling communication problem for the Church of England. Clergy who have a mind to do so can be remarkably effective in blocking communication between their parishes and the Church's central structures. In other words, a bureaucracy which creates mistrust by over-elaboration, can easily become self-defeating.

(3) A third meaning of bureaucracy identifies it with centralization

117

and 'big government'. The erosion of traditional parish autonomy and clerical independence, particularly financial independence, are two of the most obvious symptoms of a decisive shift in power. I have heard of parishes, I am glad to say not in my own diocese, where any suggestion from higher authority is automatically resisted for fear that it might be part of some diabolical plot to reorganize the parish out of existence.

Little is heard, where such fears are prevalent, about the advantages of centralization, about the fairer distribution of resources, about the wide range of central resources and services which are now in most places available to local churches. Bureaucracy becomes another name for 'big brother'.

(4) This is even more true of the fourth meaning of the word, where it is identified without qualification as a threat to liberty and individuality. The revolt against bureaucratization, understood in this fourth sense, lies at the root of a whole variety of movements and attitudes, some inside and some outside the churches. Martin has listed a few of them:[8] charismatic outbreaks; the emphasis on lay initiative; a generally undogmatic approach, except when criticisms are turned against society; eschatological and mystical yearnings; the search for tight-knit exclusive community life; contempt for church discipline and the rejection of traditional norms of conduct.

It is not suggested that the activities of Church House are themselves the cause of such manifestations. The revolt is against 'the system', in which Church House is felt to be trapped like every other institution, and which those who revolt against it believe is dehumanizing.

But this is to confuse meanings and to muddle perceptions. The reason for trying to distinguish different layers of interpretation of the word 'bureaucracy' is just to avoid this kind of muddle and the exaggerated responses which flow from it. Bureaucracy conceived as a neutral instrument is very different from the sinister force envisaged by those who find themselves at the wrong end of the bureaucratic machine.

It remains true, as pointed out in chapter 1, that there are secularizing tendencies in the existence of bureaucracy itself, however it is interpreted. To that extent Christians are right to feel

8   Martin, *The Dilemmas of Contemporary Religion* (1978), p. 41.

uneasy about ever giving it an unqualified welcome. But sweeping condemnations and sweeping reforms seldom produce the desired result. Those who abolish structures all too quickly find themselves faced with the problem of creating new ones. The practical questions are usually questions of degree, How? and How much? Given that bureaucracy can bring, indeed has brought, great benefits in making churches viable as institutions in the modern world, and given that bureaucratic organization is likely to be with us for the foreseeable future, how can it be so tempered and controlled as not to obscure the distinctive character of church life and of the Christian message? How can the three sinister aspects of bureaucracy be kept in their place? In particular, what can the central bodies of the Church of England do to counteract some of the more undesirable side-effects of their present systems?

In my article on 'Directions for the Church of England' I referred to the need to build up the confidence and autonomy of local churches, and was promptly taken to task for encouraging parochialism. I admit the danger. I acknowledge the important role played by central structures in broadening the horizons of those whose Christian vision may be deplorably limited. As a bishop I am only too well aware of the entrenched attitude of some congregations towards changes which, to those who propose them, seem clearly rational and highly desirable. But who exists for who's sake? All too often, it seems to me, local churches are made to feel that they exist for the sake of larger bodies. Talk about 'the diocese' as the basic unit of the church, while it may have a sound theological rationale, can seem very threatening to those whose actual experience of Christianity is rooted in a particular place and among particular people, and for whom 'the diocese' is an abstraction.

Obviously there are cultural differences to be taken into account here. I write from a diocese where the sense of 'place' is very strong. In other settings 'local' may not necessarily mean 'parochial', and in an increasingly mobile society patterns of Christian allegiance may well become more and more varied. Daniel Jenkins,[9] following Leslie Paul, sees three types of setting in which Christians of the future will find their church life, and which he labels 'cathedrals', 'conventicles' and 'chaplaincies'. There is a need for big occasions,

9   Daniel Jenkins, *The British*, p. 194. See also Leslie Paul's *A Church by Daylight*.

for some large-scale focus for commitment, some visible reminder of the universal church; there is also a need for face-to-face groups, Christian cells of all kinds in which faith can be nurtured. By 'chaplaincies' he infers a specific and growing ministry towards interest groups, different types of secular association which cut across neighbourhood groupings.

This is simply one possible pattern among others. But the point, which may seem so platitudinous as to be scarcely worth making, is that the small-scale does not exist for the large-scale, or vice versa. They are different and equally valid manifestations of Christian life appropriate to different contexts. Platitudes are in danger of being ignored, however, when zealous planners look at maps, and this is why one of the correctives which needs to be constantly on hand in any bureaucratic system is a prime concern for the local and the personal.

There is a classic example, in the secular sphere, of a planning failure in Sunderland, which shows how easy it is to get the balance wrong. In the early 1960s Sunderland Council had a good housing record, but when in 1965 it started a new slum clearance programme, it found its proposals resisted by about half the tenants concerned, on the grounds that they did not want to move, that their houses were perfectly adequate, and had not in any case been properly inspected. After much debate the objections were overruled, and the houses demolished 'for the good of the residents themselves'. The processes leading up to the Council's final decision were studied in detail by Norman Dennis whose subsequent book on the subject[10] is now frequently quoted to illustrate the dire effects of well-meaning central policies on those they are designed to help. He pointed out how the planners had no knowledge of the social value of the area for those who actually lived in it. Their assumption was that housing replacement was a technical matter, whereas in fact once certain obvious criteria had been met, the most important factors turned out to be personal. Dennis comments: 'There can be little sense in a policy which is justified by reference to its beneficial effects, if the 'beneficiaries' experience the results as hardship.'[11]

Ecclesiastical bureaucracies on the whole operate with a good deal of sensitivity towards their customers, and in any case generally

10   Norman Dennis, *People and Planning* (1970).
11   ibid., p. 360.

lack the kind of sanctions available to their secular counterparts. But social value and local loyalties are difficult things to handle in bureaucratic terms, which is why the temptation to undervalue them is always present.

Mary Douglas suggests another, related, way of humanizing bureaucracy:

> When bureaucrats hear the catchword 'equality', they should beware, for equality, like symmetry, is a mechanical principle in its operation. It chops the human diversity of need into its own preordained regularities. The way to humanize the system is to cherish particular categories. The institution which runs by strict adherence to general rules gives up its own autonomy. If it tries to adopt equality or seniority or alphabetical order or any other hard and fast principle for promotion or admission, it is bound to over-ride the hard case. Furthermore it is bound to abandon its traditions and so its identity and its original, special purposes. For these humanizing influences depend upon a continuity with the past, benevolent forms of nepotism, irregular charity, extraordinary promotions, freedom to pioneer in the tradition of the founders. . . .[12]

This cherishing of variety and irregularity used to be much more common in the Church of England than it is now. One of the valuable powers still left to bishops is just this possibility of introducing flexibility into the working of the machine, without having to be answerable for what is done. The tendency at synodical level, however, is to produce 'across the board' solutions to problems[13] on the assumption that variety will on the whole diminish, and ought to be encouraged to do so. The late, and unlamented, Benefices Measure was an example of this kind of legislation, which in the end fell foul of the instinct that it is better to preserve a few idiosyncrasies, than to replace personal links between parishes and their patrons with a new bureaucracy.

Another way of humanizing bureaucracy is by keeping open the realm of personal and local choice. I have already referred to the importance of this in chapter 5, in discussing folk religion. I was concerned there to make the point that one way of responding to

12 Douglas, *Natural Symbols*, p. 188.
13 Giles Hunt, 'The Church: Two Points of View' in *Theology* LXXXIII (1980) pp. 257–62.

the pressures of folk religion is to make and go on making a deliberate choice to take it seriously. There is in practice a huge difference between parishes where the clergy, whether by conviction or by temperament, lay themselves open to all-comers – and find themselves torn between ministering to their congregation and to outsiders – and parishes whose active members have themselves consciously decided to be a church 'for everybody', and so welcome the attention given to the whole community.

The same can be true of bureaucratic decisions. The decision to close a church, for instance, should almost always in my view be taken by the parishioners themselves. It may take a long time. It may involve applying certain pressures, like the refusal of capital assistance. It may lead to a situation in which parishioners *ask* for somebody else to take the final decision. But in the end this forcing of the decision on the people most affected by it, is a potent symbol of the way in which bureaucracy should serve the ends of local Christian communities, rather than dictate them.

Small correctives of this kind to patterns of bureaucratic control can in practice make a considerable difference to the feel of an organization. I suspect that similar correctives to the mode of operation of the Church of England's General Synod might be equally beneficial, and I therefore want to end this chapter by making a few practical suggestions.

The Synod is frequently accused of being unrepresentative. Various analyses[14] of membership reveal the grisly truth that it is predominantly middle-class, middle-aged, middle-of-the-road, male and white. It is difficult to see how it could be otherwise. Attempts were made, for example, before the creation of the Church Assembly, to build in a specific working-class representation.[15] But how could this be done without setting up a horrifying symbol of class division at the centre of the church's life? It is often claimed that less frequent meetings at more convenient times would encourage greater working-class participation. I doubt whether an analysis of the membership of deanery and diocesan synods would support this contention. This is not to say that working-class people are not concerned about the church. Many are. It is simply that the role

14   George Moyser, 'Patterns of Representation in the Elections to the General Synod in 1975' in *Crucible* (April 1979) and 'The 1980 General Synod: Patterns and Trends' in *Crucible* (April 1982).

15   Thompson, p. 170.

assigned to representatives in a synodical system is uncongenial to them.

The same is true of young people. The kind of experience and application required of those who want to take an active part in the complexities of synodical government is comparatively rare among young people, and by the time they have worked themselves up through the system, they are no longer young.

And so one might go on. A body such as the Synod inevitably attracts those who like that sort of thing. If its membership is unrepresentative in the sense of being untypical, it is because meeting in Synod is itself an untypical activity. Only ecclesiastical activists, or those with a particular axe to grind, are likely to have the commitment required to learn how to wield synodical power. The same is true of Parliament, which is just as short of young, black, working-class, women members as the Synod. But what does representation mean? Surely it ought not to mean that a representative body is somehow a mirror image of the society it represents, but that it is *in touch* with that society, and so can represent its opinions.

The key question, therefore, is not *who* is elected to the Synod? but *how* do representatives relate to those who elected them? On this score I believe there is a real case for some modification of the present system. This could mean having constituencies somewhat smaller than a diocese; or at least ensuring that after their election Synod members relate to particular geographical areas where they take steps to make themselves accessible and accountable.

A further step in opening up the synodical system to a wider variety of people might be at the level of boards, committees and other bodies, where much more deliberate attention could be given to the balance of age, skills and experience. The present assumption is that Synod members themselves must form the backbone of these other bodies, but there is scope for adjustment without compromising the principle of accountability to the Synod itself. One of the many drawbacks in a complicated many-layered system is that the same people have to be involved at many different levels, with the result that responsibility comes to rest more and more on a comparatively small group of activists.[16] More extensive co-option to

16 Betty Ridley, 'Government and Leadership in the Church' in *Theology* LXXXI (1978), pp. 190–5.

some of the sub-structures from right outside this circle offers a practical way of involving different categories and classes of people.

These are small adjustments, well within the limit of present possibilities, but cumulatively they might make the charge of un-representativeness less convincing.

The actual procedures of the Synod could also benefit from some adjustments, not least in the realm of Standing Orders, to which reference has already been made as an example of steady bureau-cratic growth. As those who know the Synod from within will testify, its worst moments are when it finds itself locked in a procedural straitjacket. Sometimes this is on a comparatively minor point, and there is a certain wry amusement to be found in the ingenious contortions of the experts as they try to extricate it. But sometimes the results are more serious, and it could be argued that it was procedural rigidities which, as much as anything, tipped the balance in the rejection of the Covenanting proposals.

The usual response to defects of this kind, when they become apparent, is yet further elaboration of the Standing Orders. Hence the creeping growth. But this way of dealing with problems, by the endless refinement of rules, in the long run only tightens the straitjacket. A better way, and a way which would contribute more to humanizing the system, would be to increase the discretionary powers of the presidents and chairmen.

This sounds like a dangerous suggestion, creeping authoritarian-ism as an alternative to legalistic paralysis. But once again it is a question of balance, and at present all the weight is on the side of the rule-makers. Chairmanship tends to be weak, not necessarily through personal deficiencies in the chairmen themselves, but be-cause when difficulties arise the powers of the chair are usually so limited that it is unable to take effective action.

A corollary of the proposal that discretionary powers should be increased, is that the actual chairman should be seen to have some personal authority. The present system whereby almost any mem-ber of the Synod might find him- or herself on the panel of chairmen, and then be asked to exercise an authority which relates only to chairmanship of a particular debate, while admirably democratic in theory, means that only very exceptional people can wield an authority which is instantly recognized. The alternative would be to confine the chairmanship to those who are already seen to possess authority, namely to bishops and to the elected chairmen of the different synodical Houses.

This would not be popular, particularly among the bishops themselves. But it is the kind of change which, if brought about with understanding, would not only have procedural advantages, but also might help the Synod to think of itself more on a churchly, and less on a parliamentary, model. It would also be a visible symbol of the interweaving of the democratic and the hierarchical systems, which the Synod still lacks in the day-to-day management of its business.

A final example of the kind of adjustment which might help the Synod to discover its proper churchly character concerns synodical 'pronouncements'. Reference was made in chapter 3 to the difficulties encountered when a church as a whole tries to say something on controversial matters.[17] A body like the Synod is much better at legitimating views, at demonstrating by open debate where the range of Christian conviction lies, than in committing itself convincingly to a single plan of action. The famous debate on *The Church and the Bomb* was significant *as a debate*, and rightly gained attention because it was topical, well-prepared, and showed a more serious grasp of the issues than much of the popular political debate on the subject. The motion eventually agreed is likely to be forgotten long before the debate itself, because it is no more than one statement among many in a long-running process of public discussion.

What the Synod has to offer on such topics is a distinctive *quality* of debate, a distinctive appreciation of the religious dimension in public affairs, rather than a distinctive set of answers. Its rational democratic structure, however, tempts it into believing that it can do more than this, that the essential thing is not to think things through in a responsibly-minded Christian context, but to secure a vote deploring this or that, or urging the Government to take some highly improbable action.

The procedural danger-points are usually private members' motions. Some of these invite instant decisions on controversial topics, debated without any proper preparation or documentation, and frequently worded in such a way as to make the Synod look foolish if it says yes, and curmudgeonly if it says no. This is harsh criticism, so it is important to stress that it is criticism of a procedure, not

17   page 60.

criticism of the rights of individual members to put forward ideas from the floor. The question, like all others, is a question of balance. How can ideas be received and rights safeguarded without the Synod being trapped in a system which encourages snap and superficial judgements? Off-the-cuff pronouncements devalue all pronouncements. The formation of a Christian mind takes time. When the Church speaks, it ought to speak seriously.

An obvious way of redressing the balance might be to adopt the procedure already followed in the House of Lords. There individual members have the right to initiate debates on any subject and, as the standard form of motion puts it, 'ask for papers'. At the conclusion of such a debate there is no vote, and the request for papers is invariably withdrawn. It is the debate itself which matters. If the subject is important, and if the debate has warranted it, action may follow in some other appropriate context. In synodical terms, the next step might be for the Standing Committee or one of the boards to mount a properly documented debate. Procedurally this would be more complicated than the present arrangements, and to this extent the proposal runs counter to my previous arguments. But the key question is what kind of body does the Synod understand itself to be? And when it speaks, what kind of authority does it want to attach to its statements? The idea that it is the 'church's parliament' which can say what it likes when it likes, shows its inadequacy at this point because the existing procedures by-pass any notion of 'government' responsibility. There is no corrective to a sudden vote in a thin house on a motion whose full implications may not have been seen.

These last pages may seem to have been occupied with small matters of concern only to a very limited group of people. Who worries about such synodical minutiae? A chapter which started by exalting aims over processes and by turning attention to large-scale sociological interpretations, has narrowed down to a detailed discussion of procedures in a body which is in any case tempted to over-inflate its own importance.

The rake's progress has been deliberate. 'He who would do good to another must do it in minute particulars,'[18] applies just as much to organizations as to individuals. The fact that it was a visionary, William Blake, who said it, ought to be some guarantee that there

18 From Blake's *Jerusalem*.

is no necessary opposition between the kinds of vision without which people perish, and the kinds of detail without which nothing gets done.

Those who know the Church of England from within, who see her strengths and deplore her weakness, who see the immensity of the task to be done if the Gospel is to be preached faithfully to this generation, who are conscious of resources being wasted and opportunities missed, who know only too well the rigidities and anomalies in her structure, are sometimes tempted to stand up and prophesy against her. But this may be an easy way out. Anybody can make sweeping condemnations of bureaucracy, or rage against 'the system', or advocate radical changes to everything in general.

In the real world more progress is often made, though with less noise, by those who decide carefully in which direction they ought to move, and then set off one step at a time.

8

Alternative Worship

On the 8th of April 1981 both Houses of Parliament debated the Prayer Book Protection Bill, a Private Member's Bill designed to secure regular use of the Book of Common Prayer at a main service once a month in churches where twenty or more parishioners requested it. The debate in the Commons was brief, though heated. In the Lords the benches were crowded, there was a huge list of speakers, members from the Commons packed into the space allowed them in the Chamber, many harsh things were said, and the vote was finally taken at 12.50 a.m. in a, by then, much reduced House. The Bill was given a second reading in both Houses, and thereafter by mutual consent passed into oblivion.

It was an absurd Bill, as most of its supporters recognized. It would have been unworkable. It trespassed on dangerous ground in the relationship between Church and State, and warnings to this effect were given both by the Church and by the Government. But it served as a protest. It focused worries about what were seen as reckless changes in the Church of England, and particular fears about the long-term effects of the publication of the Alternative Service Book. An earlier petition to safeguard the use of the Prayer Book, signed by a large number of distinguished people,[1] and backed up by a collection of critical essays, had apparently fallen on deaf ears when presented to the General Synod. The Bill was therefore seen as a last ditch attempt by the laity to frustrate what many of its supporters were convinced was a clerical plot.

The debate itself was mostly superficial. Its importance lies in the fact that it took place at all. Parliamentary concern about the details of worship may seem strange in a nation which has gone so far in the direction of secular pluralism, but is evidence that secu-

1 *P.N. Review* 13, *Crisis for Cranmer and King James* (1979).

larization is by no means complete. There are those, both Christian and non-Christian, who are not content for the Church of England to become a private institution, and who still want it to be the church of the English people and one of the guardians of English culture. And Parliament still wants, in however minimal a sense, to go on regarding itself as the voice of the laity. Despite the unease which such sentiments can generate in some Christian minds, therefore, and despite the sabre-rattling about disestablishment, there was a positive message in the debate which is central to the theme of this book. As the bishop who happened to be on the receiving end of much of the criticism, I found a certain paradoxical comfort in the fact that such feelings were being expressed. It was sad, though, to find little real comprehension of the complexity of the issues. In my own speech I put it thus:

> Those of us who stand at the centre of it have the problem, first of all, of trying to maintain viable congregations of committed people in an age when commitment has to be strong and lively if it is to be of service at all; and generally it is those strong and lively people at the centre of church life who get elected to its councils and, ultimately, to the Synod. But alongside that problem of maintaining lively communities we have, secondly, the problem of remaining faithful to the past in an age which is radically different from that in which the church was originally shaped. Thirdly we have the problem in the Church of England of trying to retain our links with the half-committed and occasionally interested and the folk religionists. And, fourthly, we have the problem of trying to reach out towards those for whom our cultural heritage means little or nothing. In trying to balance these four things we, as bishops, are well aware that we are having to indulge in a very difficult juggling act because many of these goals conflict with one another.[2]

The debate about worship, in other words, leads straight to fundamental questions about the church's understanding of itself and its task, and its relation to the nation. Conservative defenders of the Book of Common Prayer are not to be dismissed as cranks or mere antiquarians, even if they do sometimes speak more stridently and self-confidently than the facts warrant. Stupid things

2 *Hansard*, no. 1142, pp. 625–6.

have been said on both sides, sometimes rude and hurtful and even untrue things, and there has been little appreciation in some quarters of the actual dilemmas faced by clergy working among those for whom the traditional language of worship seems almost totally foreign. It was particularly unfortunate that the General Synod's only reported response to the Prayer Book petition was in an intemperate speech on a different subject by a young clergyman more renowned for his articulateness than for his wisdom. He appealed in demagogic fashion to the Synod's dislike of being pushed around, and won his due measure of publicity. The much resented lack of any formal response was at least partly the result of the procedural rigidity of the Synod, which found itself nonplussed by having nothing in its ubiquitous Standing Orders to cover so unusual an event. My own attempt at a later stage in the session to make some conciliatory remarks, went largely unheeded.

Mutual suspicion of an unhealthy kind still persists, some based on genuine differences of opinion, but some fed unnecessarily by the highly charged atmosphere in which public discussion has taken place. It is therefore important to try to identify the key issues and see whether there is a more constructive way to proceed in the future. To keep the discussion within bounds, I shall confine my remarks to the major criticisms of the Alternative Service Book (A.S.B.) as set out in the book of essays, *No Alternative*,[3] and in the earlier critical essays which preceded its publication and were presented with the Synod petition.

The criticisms fall into four main categories. Most obvious and most vehement are attacks on the language of the new services. This is described as banal, uninspired, lacking poetry, neither modern nor ancient but quasi-modern with occasional archaisms. Critics ask why it was necessary to change so much that was well-known, well-loved, beautiful and not difficult to understand, and point to the disastrous loss of numinous sense when religion ceases to use a special language for worship. The change from 'thou' to 'you' in addressing God, while distasteful to many in itself, has had the secondary effect of triggering off widespread grammatical reconstructions. Monstrosities like 'you who' are fortunately rare, but the circumlocutions designed to avoid them frequently create a sense of

3 David Martin and Peter Mullen (ed.), *No Alternative: The Prayer Book Controversy* (1981).

jerkiness. The Collects have suffered particularly in this respect; indeed they are commonly accused of being the weakest part of the book.

This criticism of language shades into a second realm of criticism which could be called broadly sociological. Martin has written extensively on the undesirable consequences of liturgical change itself, on the loss of corporate memory entailed by it and the up-rooting of what he calls 'boundary markers'. The maintenance of personal and ecclesiastical identity depends on continuities of which language, when it has sunk deeply into the mind and culture of a people, is one of the main carriers. His argument would be a strong one even if he approved aesthetically of the changes which have taken place. As it is, he sees poor workmanship conspiring with gratuitous destructiveness to cut away the roots of English culture. He puts liturgical revision firmly in the context of the other developments discussed throughout this book: 'The new texts can be seen as part of several shifts: to sectarianism and mandatory communality, to the ecclesiastical multinational and bureaucratic governance.'[4]

The point is taken even further by one of his fellow-sociologists who writes:

> Although liturgical acts are not secular, liturgical change secularizes liturgies in the same way that criticism erodes the authority of all texts . . . The lay worshipper becomes a lay critic of the liturgical text during periods of liturgical revision. 'Where today shall we put the Gloria, do you suppose?' . . . Once the wholeness of the liturgy is a matter for critical reflection rather than a taken-for-granted order, the reality expressed and established in the liturgy also comes into question.[5]

I suspect that this is an example of pushing an argument to the point of absurdity. To remove critical consciousness from worship altogether is to fall into a kind of idolatry, a liturgical fundamentalism which in its extreme forms is just as stultifying as liturgical dilettantism. But the general direction of the argument is interesting and important. What has been said in earlier chapters about the consequences of widening the realm of choice in religion, can be

4 *P.N. Review* 13, p. 2.
5 R. K. Fenn, 'The Political Dimension of the Liturgy' in *P.N. Review* 13, p. 14.

just as significant at the microscopic as at the macroscopic level, at the level of liturgy as at the level of denominationalism. Facetious comments about the number of permutations and combinations possible in the A.S.B. take on a more serious dimension if it is true that religious choice itself is a mark of secularization.

A third area of criticism is theological and ecclesiological. It is claimed that there has been a distinct shift of theological emphasis in the new services, a flight from the ruggedness and directness of the Prayer Book with its deep consciousness of sin, its ability to convey the sense of God's transcendence, and its invitation to personal commitment. All this is in sharp contrast to the A.S.B. which is seen as fundamentally a 'church book', community-orientated, more concerned with celebration than with penitence, with 'God-in-the-midst' than with transcendent holiness. The prime symbol of the transformation is the exchange of the 'Peace' in the middle of the eucharist. For some it is a joyful celebration of togetherness, and there are charismatic churches where the hugging and kissing can interrupt the main flow of the service for ten minutes or more; for others it is an embarrassing distraction, an intrusion of human banality at the very moment when the worshipper most wants to be aware of God.

In by far the most perceptive essay in *No Alternative*,[6] Vanstone has written about the needs of different people and different churches at different times. Sometimes a church needs to provide what he calls 'place'. Our 'place' is where we belong, where we feel at home, where our personal concerns are seen to be important and can be shared. A style of worship which encourages this sense of belonging together may be essential for building up confidence in contexts where Christian commitment is weak and community life unable to sustain a religious dimension. Its danger lies in excluding those whose needs are different, or who are not at home in the 'place' provided for others, or who are ready to grow beyond their 'place' if they are given 'space' to do so.

'Space' in worship entails restraint, distance, a measure of privacy, an awareness that there are dimensions beyond the particular needs which may have brought a worshipper to church. When, as easily happens in modern liturgies, the celebrant dominates the occasion by his power to choose and particularize and force a sense

6   Martin and Mullen (ed.), p. 143 seq.

of community, the net effect may well be a diminution of the worshippers' 'space'. A detailed intercession, for instance, full of individual petitions may speak clearly to some, while forcing others to
feel alienated and bereft. Compulsory fellowship may support and
encourage some, while reminding others of their emotional exclusion. Endless exchanges of the 'Peace' every time Christians worship
together, can introduce a note of falsity into a ceremony which in
the right place and on the right occasion can be a dramatic sign of
mutual discovery and reconciliation. Prayer Book worship, by its
very distance from ordinary life, and by subordinating the celebrant
to the liturgy, allows space for those who need it.

Martin takes up a related theme in referring to the threshold the
worshipper has to cross if the act of worship is to rise above mere
celebration of human feelings and experiences. Special buildings,
special actions, special words mark the transition from every-day
life into a world of otherness, holiness, transcendence. Remove the
markers, lower the barriers, and the transition no longer takes place.

> The jingles of the new liturgy and guitar music may have a place
> when it comes to creating camaraderie, but they allow no ap-
> proach to the *mysterium tremendum*. All the rich deposits of music
> and speech which evoke the transcendent, mark out the religious
> mode of being and mediate the divine presence are being eroded
> in favour of an empoverished sectarianism and a clerically or-
> chestrated conviviality. Those who have done this think they are
> reaching out to the world of the every-day and the modern. This
> is why they have the impudence to present their sham antique as
> modern. In fact they have reached *out* to nothing, least of all the
> world. They have simply reached *down* to the mundane.[7]

Underneath the rhetoric, there is a valid point being made. But
what if the barriers between the mundane and the transcendent
seem so high to those who are not used to crossing them, that they
never even try? How does one draw the line between churches and
liturgies which feel sacred, and those which feel merely foreign?
Vanstone has a better balance than Martin here, and points the
way to a genuine reconciliation between different styles and traditions. Clergy sensitive enough to combine both 'place' and 'space'
stand some chance of making worship both accessible and profound.

7   ibid., p. 20.

The fourth main area of criticism is political. Supporters of the Prayer Book constantly assert that they are not wishing to abolish the A.S.B., despite many contemptuous things said about it. Their plea is for fairness, for the Prayer Book to be given its due place, to remain as it were in the bloodstream of the church, without being squeezed out and forgotten. They suspect a concerted effort by bishops, theological colleges and clergy in general, to force new liturgies on unwilling congregations, and even when persuaded that there is no deliberate plot, they see a church in which the process of change is out of control and can only be halted by some drastic action. Running through this strand of criticism is a latent anti-clericalism, still very modest by continental standards, but accentuated by the new liturgical dominance of the clergy, to which Vanstone draws attention. Mutterings about 'trendy vicars' are probably in many cases quite unjust, but they reveal an insecurity about what the vicar might possibly get up to, which is one of the symptoms of living in a time of rapid change. The consciousness of change itself, the complexity of decision-making processes and the multifariousness of the choices, all put more power in the hands of the professionals. It is hardly surprising that many lay people feel threatened, and interpret the threat as if it were a conspiracy.

These four areas of criticism are not, of course, distinct from one another. I have separated them for convenience, but in practice linguistic, sociological, theological and political factors are all interwoven in most actual critical comments. Together they make a formidable case which needs to be heard and understood, and might be much more sympathetically received if it were presented less polemically. This is one reason for spelling it out in some detail in this chapter.

To try to answer the case would require a book in itself, even if I were interested in merely trying to refute it. The fact is that there are genuine Christian insights on both sides of the arguments, and the practical problem is how to combine them, not how to prove that one side or the other is wrong.

Liturgical revision has a long history. It grew out of dissatisfaction with existing forms, and clergy who remember when 1662, and only 1662, comprised the total liturgical diet may well recall the sense of impoverishment and frustration it could generate, particularly on occasions which needed some special marker, beyond a bare change of collect, epistle and gospel. In the days when I started as a curate, there was growing liturgical anarchy. The frustrations were felt more deeply by the clergy than by the laity because, whereas the laity can let a service wash over them, clergy have to concentrate on the actual words, and find more and more strain in having to say words which they have ceased to regard as appropriate. To this extent critics of liturgical revision who dismiss it as clerically inspired have some truth on their side.

But what are clergy to do? There is a proper clerical concern with meaning and if, as is bound to happen, meanings and emphases change in the course of theological and social development, there comes a time when these changes have to receive some liturgical expression. Clergy thus find themselves caught between a thoroughly understandable desire for stability and an equally understandable desire to represent more fully what they actually believe. There are dangers in all this; dangers in succumbing to fashion; dangers in losing meaning rather than gaining it; dangers in substituting 'meaningfulness' for meaning, where 'meaningfulness' has more to do with tricks of style, presentation, emphasis etc., than depth of insight; above all there is the danger of forgetting that the ultimate meaning of liturgical words and actions is mysterious, and that liturgical language should carry markers to make clear its function in pointing beyond itself.[8]

I do not pretend that these dangers have all been avoided in the process of liturgical revision which led up to the A.S.B. But neither do I think that the pressures to undertake revision could have been avoided or redirected. The fact that from the start liturgical revision has been both international and interdenominational is evidence that it is not the peculiar quirk of a few English churchmen.

To those involved in it, it has been a movement of the spirit, a process of discovery and renewal. Hostile critics may talk of world-wide surrender to the passing spirit of the age. Whichever interpretation is chosen, or whatever mixture of the two, the strength of the forces at work can hardly be doubted. Critics have to ask themselves whether the rapid dissemination of alternative forms of worship could ever have taken place if the old forms had really been regarded as adequate. Clerical dominance can hardly be the total explanation.

8   See I.T. Ramsey, *Religious Language* (1957). Ramsey's work on religious language needs to be given more attention in the field of liturgy than it has so far received.

The scene was thus set, and the Liturgy of the Church of South India was one of the catalysts which encouraged many people to look for a new richness, a new flexibility and a new theological balance in worship, appropriate to a hopeful new era. The fact that it came from the first major united church in the world was not insignificant. Was this fashion? Or was God genuinely doing new things?

The actual course of liturgical revision in this country fulfilled some of these hopes and disappointed others. It is not my intention to tell the story. I have already written about one small part of it which I was privileged to witness from the inside,[9] and have tried to express something of the sheer difficulty of wrestling with language in the context of the appallingly cumbersome procedures which the Church of England is legally bound to operate. My final comment that, given the procedures, the result was about the best that could be expected, was neither meant to damn with faint praise nor to signal unqualified approval. There *are* mistakes and banalities and unnecessary tinkerings, and I shall return to some of these later. But whatever the critics say, the new services have in fact brought new life and meaning into the worship of thousands of churches. This is an everyday experience for those whose job takes them into many different places of worship, and this is why church leaders are apt to react a little impatiently to those who write so eloquently about spiritual impoverishment.

Faced with this explosion of interest and experiment, the Synod's decision to publish the A.S.B. should be seen as a conservative measure rather than as a further incitement to change. Those of us who planned the book saw the need for a period of stability and reflection, time for new texts to become familiar and to reveal how well they stood up to repeated use. Concentration on the book created a natural pause. It was deliberately designed as an opportunity for the Church of England to catch up with itself and assess what it had done. I was also myself particularly concerned not to let slip the Anglican habit or worshipping from a book owned by church members themselves, and available at home. It is a habit which could easily have died after ten years of worshipping from pamphlets, and I was conscious of the need to move quickly even

9 John Habgood, 'On Being a Liturgical Reviser' in *Theology* LXXXII (1979), pp. 95–102.

if this meant producing a book with a limited life. In fact the limited life was itself seen as an advantage. It is a guarantee that the period of assessment is genuinely intended to be just that, and it is in my mind a genuinely open question whether the next revision will be in a more radical or a more conservative direction.

The size and complexity of the resulting book have been frequent subjects for attack, but it has not often been noticed that these are themselves evidence of the desire to stabilize and familiarize. The most bulky part of the A.S.B., the collects and lessons for Holy Communion, contain more than three times as much material as the B.C.P. It was decided, however, to print them in full in order to encourage the use of standard biblical texts, and hence in some measure to counteract the loss of familiarity brought about by the multitude of modern biblical translations. The printing of the actual texts is also intended to help clergy use the new translations intelligently, selecting those which are best for reading particular passages aloud, and sticking closer to the Authorized Version in the famous passages read on the great festivals.

The complexity of the A.S.B. is in part a measure of the complexity of the present-day world. Seventy-two pages of initiation services may seem excessive, when the B.C.P. managed with services for infant baptism and confirmation, and one for use with natives on the plantations. The new services nevertheless represent pastoral realities, and the complexities are intended to bring order into an otherwise chaotic area of liturgical private enterprise. Despite sarcastic references by critics to the language of Income Tax returns, the complex rubrics do in fact serve the cause of stability.

The plethora of alternatives in the Holy Communion services has much less justification, but it is important to refute the suggestion that it is merely a symptom of divisions in churchmanship. The problem is rather one of *embarras de richesse*, and an unwillingness to jettison promising ideas until they have been tested. The hope is that in a subsequent revision it will become clear what can be pruned away without loss.

The churchmanship issue is, of course, highly relevant to the Holy Communion services, but in this respect the gains produced by revision have been immense. For the first time this century all members of the Church of England, of whatever churchmanship, can now worship together using the same words without feeling dishonest or deprived in doing so. This was not true of the Prayer Book.

Internationally and ecumenically, too, there have been great gains. In the days of empire it was possible to conceive of African and Indian villagers, even at one stage American colonists, remaining stubbornly faithful to Cranmer. But there is no way in which autonomous and growing churches in independent nations could have been held fixed in a pattern of worship which owed nothing to their own cultural development. The fact that the inevitable changes formed part of a worldwide movement, has allowed churches to demonstrate their freedom without a disastrous slide into total disunity and chaos. In years to come it seems likely that the kind of balance which the Church of England has managed to find in its own worship will be a factor aiding convergence. Indeed there are already forces at work through the international links between liturgical scholars, which encourage convergence and set limits to further liturgical fragmentation. Even now, though precise words may differ, the preferred shape of the revised Eucharist is almost universal in the major traditions.

Shape is one thing, though, and words are another. All that has been said so far about the pressures for change might be conceded, and the intentions underlying the publication of the A.S.B. might be approved, but why did the language have to be changed? And why did the changes have to be so radical and so apparently destructive? In this question we reach the heart of the complaints.

I believe two forces have been at work here, one relatively superficial, and the other much more deeply rooted in some of the problems of our present culture.

Those who criticize the process of liturgical revision as an unstoppable bandwagon have grasped a partial truth. One change leads to another, in the interests of consistency. Many of the minor changes which so irritate those who hear the echo of familiar phrases, have been made, not in the interests of clarity or poetry, nor because anybody is so foolish as to think that the new version is better than the old, but simply because the new and the old do not easily mix. It is the necessity for new writing, new services or parts of services, or new emphases in existing services, which raises most sharply the question of the appropriate liturgical language for the twentieth century. The question would be less sharp if it had been sufficient to take existing liturgies and do a little invisible mending. But supposing revision needs to go further than this, how is it to be done? Is it possible with integrity to produce new Cranmerian prose? Or must the prior existence of this body of superb language set limits to what all subsequent generations can actually say and do?

The impulse to use new language is, as I see it, an inevitable consequence of the belief that there are new things to be said. All sorts of additional reasons have been given for it, from claims that it is more 'meaningful', to claims that modernity itself is good. But fundamentally it is a question of integrity. Honest prayer and honest writing must belong to the culture in which they are born. Once born, the rest follows; the new language, created for certain key purposes, begins to clothe itself in a total environment. All sorts of other things which, seen in isolation, are not in need of change, are swept into the process.

But what if modern culture cannot carry the load of meaning liturgical language should bear? With this question we begin to touch on the deeper forces which have made liturgical revision both necessary and impossible. Mary Douglas, as so often, can provide a helpful clue. In an illuminating discussion of anti-ritualism she traces its source to patterns of society in which social bonds are weak and social structures are fluid. Societies and families which thrive on 'openness', which exalt sensitivity to feelings and self-expression over particuar roles and relationships, make it difficult for those brought up in them to experience any sense of pattern in life, or constraint over it.

> The causes of anti-ritualism today in middle-class European and American communities would appear to be a predictable result of a process of socialization in which the child never internalizes a pattern of social statuses and never experiences authoritative control which exalts the self-evident property of a social system to command obedience. Symbols of solidarity and hierarchy have not been part of his education. Consequently a form of aesthetic experience is closed to him.[10]

If a family never eats together, but follows the pattern of early supper for one, choir practice for another, a snack from the freezer for a third, how can it begin to understand the ritual overtones of

10   Douglas, *Natural Symbols*, p. 55.

the Eucharist? How can those who have never experienced a beneficent authority in school or family, make an appropriate emotional response to authoritative words and gestures? Nor is this ritual poverty just a by-product of middle-class liberal values and life styles; the general thrust of our society, particularly its anti-authoritarianism and its fragmentation, erodes the capacity to benefit from strong public symbolism.

The same applies to language. The inaccessibility of exalted liturgical language to many people is not a matter of incomprehension. Those who say that it is perfectly possible to learn the meaning of unfamiliar words miss the point. The problem is emotional inaccessibility, the fact that a certain style of language can 'feel wrong', because the constraints needed to enter into it with emotional integrity have been lacking.

The same point was noted by Wilkinson in relation to the language of war.[11] No doubt the reasons why heroic military rhetoric, in the style familiar at the beginning of the First World War, nowadays sounds artificial and embarrassing, has more to do with growing realism about war than with anti-ritualism. But the distrust of expansive and eloquent language runs right the way through our present society. Churches can, and should, swim against the stream as a witness to their distinctiveness, but even in the most traditional churches certain kinds of rhetoric would nowadays feel hopelessly out of place.

There is no simple way of finding appropriate liturgical expression in an unheroic and anti-ritualistic age. The point was made earlier that it is both necessary and impossible; there are therefore bound to be disappointments. It would be foolish to claim that the language of the A.S.B. provides the kind of bridge between contemporary speech and richer forms of language, which our age seems to need. I have already admitted that it is full of mistakes, banalities and imperfections. But those who criticize it for being an uneasy mixture between the contemporary and the faintly archaic, have been misled by the unwise claims to modernity, and have failed to see that some such mixture was inevitable. The problem, and there is no real answer to it yet, is how to find the right balance between language which feels different enough to signal that it is doing a

11 Wilkinson, *The Church of England and the First World War*, p. 172.

more than ordinary job, and which is still familiar enough not to create an inhibiting sense of artificiality.

There is an instructive parallel with the way in which liturgies are actually spoken. A good delivery is neither conversational nor totally impersonal, but somewhere in between. The key to it is disciplined emotion, and restrained involvement. One of the dangers of modern liturgies is that they tempt clergy into an over-conversational style which, added to innumerable 'helpful' interruptions, is the surest way of making them sound absurd and feel ungodly. In fact I suspect that some of the vehemence about A.S.B. language stems more from experiences of this kind than from the actual words themselves. Well delivered, much of the phraseology can carry a remarkable depth of meaning, and gradually develop its own resonances.

Before leaving the question of language, it is worth noting that the most heavily criticized parts of the A.S.B. have frequently been the so-called ICET and ICEL texts. These are internationally produced versions of historic liturgical items, such as the canticles, creeds and gloria, which are common to a large part of the Christian world. In theory it was an admirable idea to promote Christian unity by trying to ensure that most churches undertook to use the same words at central points in their worship. In practice the compromises entailed in international negotiations have produced versions which bear the stamp of their committee origin even more heavily than other parts of the liturgy.

One of the chief victims of the process has been the Lord's Prayer, now in its third revision. The most recent change, the reinsertion of the clause 'lead us not into temptation', was authorised by the General Synod unexpectedly and unilaterally, with the result that the Church of England now has its own unique version which is neither traditional, nor international, nor modern. Of the three most difficult features in the traditional version – the word 'hallowed', the word 'trespasses', and the idea that God might lead us into temptation – two remain, and the third – 'trespasses' – has been retranslated 'sins'. This weakens the word by implying that human beings can sin against one another, whereas strictly it applies first and foremost to our relationship with God. In my speech in the 1981 debate in the House of Lords I described the present version of the prayer as 'a mess'. And that is exactly what it is.

It is ironic that when Christians now meet ecumenically or internationally, the only version of the Lord's Prayer which all can say together is the traditional one. In this respect, therefore, the principle of international co-operation has been a failure, and revision has proved to be damagingly divisive as well as linguistically inept. I believe it would do much good if the failure were to be publicly admitted, and if churches were to be encouraged to revert to the exclusive use of the traditional version.

Such a move would be a small but very significant gesture of willingness to combine the new and the old, and it is not difficult to think of other small reversions to tradition which would not only be improvements in themselves, but might also help to turn antagonism into co-operation. An example would be the use of the traditional formula during the laying-on-of-hands in the Confirmation service. Except on big occasions when time is at a premium, the present A.S.B. formula is much too abrupt.

More general ways of combining old and new run into greater difficulties, and it is to these that we must now, briefly and finally, turn. The hope expressed in the A.S.B. Preface that the book might supplement rather supersede the Book of Common Prayer, is already fulfilled in minor ways in the very large number of parishes which designate special types of service, usually Evensong and 8 o'clock Holy Communion, for Prayer Book worship. My experience in my own diocese is that a pattern of this kind is widely acceptable.

One of the main practical problems in going further than this, say by the use of the different books at main Sunday morning services, is that alternate use at the same service highlights their incompatibilities. The most obvious is the existence of two different and incompatible lectionaries. The collects, insofar as they are related to the lectionaries, constitute another problem. And there are more far-reaching problems about the ability of congregations to switch styles Sunday by Sunday, and still retain a sense of familiarity with their worship.

Future revision of the A.S.B., and a willingness on the part of B.C.P. supporters to adapt and amend, might ease the way to a compromise solution, but it would suffer from the fault of all compromises in that nobody would be really satisfied. The alternative, if the intention really is to keep both traditions alive, would be to look for a territorial solution to the problem of combining old and new, rather than to insist that everybody should have a little bit of everything; in other words, to move in the direction of greater pluralism.

It could be argued that, provided different traditions are reasonably accessible in different places, and provided they are not in competition with one another, but are seen and known as part of a single Christian body, there is no inherent reason why individual churches should not adopt one or the other tradition exclusively. Sheer pluralism *is* competitive. The present haphazard variety in the Church of England, and the eclecticism in the larger urban areas, are not good advertizements for the idea that different traditions should be represented in different places.

But suppose the pluralism were planned. I have argued in a previous chapter that the deliberate choice of an open policy towards folk religion alters the quality of response to it. In much the same way the privatizing effects of pluralism can be mitigated if it is deliberately planned as part of a larger vision of what the church might be. To put it in practical terms, there is a fundamental difference between the present haphazardness of the Church of England, where the distribution of traditions is dependent largely on chance or the whims of individual clergy, and what might be the case if decisions were taken at some appropriate level, say the deanery or part of a deanery, about representing Christian tradition in its wholeness in a given area.

Planned variety of this kind is already in operation in small measure in some team ministries, but formal team arrangements are not essential to it. Churches can work together and support one another and genuinely complement one another without being in competition, in all sorts of ways. Collaborative patterns have great advantages in a mobile age, when it is still possible for people to belong to a locality, without being confined to a single location. The important thing is to use the opportunities for collaboration as a source of spiritual enrichment, to value the different identities of churches, while encouraging awareness that to belong to one is to belong to all.

It would be foolish to pretend that such collaborative planning, aimed at securing proper variety, would be easy to achieve in the Church of England. Team ministries are difficult enough as it is. But I see no other way of trying to turn present differences in the church into strengths, or passing beyond sterile controversy about styles of worship into an actual enjoyment of human diversity.

Sometimes things are made easier by becoming more complicated and, as we shall see in the next chapter, it is possible that new efforts at local ecumenism might provide the necessary stimulus.

The overall aim, however, ought to be clear. It is to provide a 'large' environment in which individuals can find both the 'place' and the 'space' to put down roots and grow.

9

What Future for Ecumenism?

The ecumenical scene is a curious mixture of hope and disappointment. Those who take the long view can justifiably claim successes. This century has seen dramatic advances in understanding and improvements in relationships between the major Christian denominations. But unity itself, despite decades of effort and with a few honourable exceptions, remains tantalizingly elusive. Hopes are raised, only to be dashed. And even the most promising pointers to the future, of which the ARCIC[1] documents are a prime example, contain ample warnings of difficulties still ahead.

Why is unity so hard to achieve? In line with the general approach in other parts of this book, I shall not attempt to give historical or theological answers, on which there is more than enough documentation already. I want, instead, to concentrate on certain contradictions within ecumenism itself, which sociological studies have helped to identify.

Wilson's well-known analysis of the ecumenical movement as a symptom of weakness,[2] tells only part of the story, and has met severe criticism. True, there is a sense in which churches may try to find significance in relation to one another, as they lose it in relation to society. There is a sense, too, in which a willingness to submerge differences can be interpreted as one of the signs of loss of conviction. It may also be true that the more flourishing sectarian bodies tend to be less interested in ecumenism, than old-fashioned churches which are having a struggle to maintain their former commitments. But it is equally possible to claim that churches only begin to take ecumenism seriously when they feel self-confident

1 Anglican Roman Catholic International Commission. See their *Final Report* (1982).
2 Wilson, *Religion in Secular Society*, p. 128, 176, etc.

enough to face the challenges and disruptions it entails.[3] And the record of ecumenical bodies, such as the British Council of Churches or the World Council of Churches, hardly substantiates the charge of massive withdrawal into self-contained 'churchiness'. On the contrary, it is precisely ecumenism, at least in this kind of manifestation, which in the eyes of some has become dangerously political.

Other analyses are similarly incomplete. One way of interpreting convergence between Christian traditions is in terms of common response to shared social pressures. The decline in many traditional social distinctions has removed part of the support system which gave some religious divisions their social meaning. Mobility and a growing acceptance of pluralism have led to increasing contacts between religious groups. Berger picks out bureaucratization as one of the forces pushing churches into the same organizational mould.[4] The new brand of ecclesiastical administrators share the same experiences, and learn to relate easily to one another at the level where ecumenical conversations take place. Liturgical experts do the same. How far they are driven by the churches' retreat into 'religion', how far liturgical convergence is the simple fruit of theological and liturgical scholarship, a new and productive return to roots, and how far the new internationalism and easier communications have contributed to the process, are questions to which there is no easy answer. Social forces and intellectual movements are not mutually exclusive explanations.

A further interesting source of ambiguity is the role of the clergy in ecumenism. In some respects the movement is undeniably clerical. Towler observes how the clergy have many more opportunities than the laity for making religious cross-cultural contacts.[5] Though laity may mix with a greater variety of people, their contacts are not generally ones in which religion is seen to be particularly significant. Lay religion is slanted towards the personal and private, whereas clerical religion slants towards the socially explicit and professional. Clerical contacts with members of other denominations tend, therefore, to be different in kind from ordinary lay contacts, and are much more self-consciously religious.

The difference is apparent, too, in attitudes towards local

---

3 Glasner, *The Sociology of Secularization*, p. 21.
4 Berger, *The Social Reality of Religion* (1969), p. 140.
5 Towler, *Homo Religiosus*, p. 173.

churches.[6] Clergy are likely to have much less religious investment in a particular congregation or a particular church building, than laity who have not had the same opportunities to worship in other contexts, or who do not feel so securely rooted in the church at a higher organizational level. Local ecumenism can thus seem more threatening to the laity than to the clergy, especially if it is combined with talk of rationalization and conserving resources.

At other levels, however, the laity can frequently express impatience at what they see as clerical intransigence on the subject of unity, and the wearisome concentration in ecumenical negotiations on the status of the clergy themselves. Here the boot is on the other foot. At denominational level, it is the clergy who feel threatened, because it is they especially who are the guardians of the ethos and customary symbols of their tradition. Laity are more likely to take these for granted.

In even a very sketchy analysis it is thus possible to see many different strands within the ecumenical movement, and many potential sources of conflict. There are important differences between local ecumenism, and ecumenism at national and international level, which are likely to evoke different responses from clergy and laity. 'W.C.C. man', as Martin calls him,[7] is seen as belonging to a professionalized elite whose activities, especially when they take a political turn, frequently serve to widen the gulf between pastors and their flocks. The highly technical nature of much ecumenical discussion is a source of frustration and discouragement to those for whom the issues seem simple and obvious. The behaviour of different interest groups, as in the Janus-like attitude of the General Synod's House of Clergy which protests its desire for unity but turns down all concrete proposals, tends only to breed cynicism. It is hard to see how, at least in England, the particular style of ecumenical negotiation which has prevailed hitherto, can survive many more rebuffs.

At the heart of these ambiguities and contradictions lies a suspicion that the quest for unity is itself a source of disunity. Some divisions may disappear, only to reappear in different places. In the later stages of the work of the Churches Council for Covenanting, for instance, when things seemed to be going well, thought was given to the terms on which Baptists might join the covenanting

6   ibid., p. 167–8.
7   Martin, *A General Theory of Secularization*, p. 295.

process. Two things were immediately apparent: first that this would split the Baptists themselves; and secondly that the question opened up whole new areas of difficulty which, if explored, might threaten the unity already achieved. The independent tradition challenges the ecumenical movement about the *level* at which unity should be sought. What is the basis for believing that the goal ought to be a union of national churches? Might not local churches unite? And if the answer is given that local church unity would threaten the universality of the church, why stop at the national level? The same question is, of course, posed by the Roman Catholic church, though from a totally different perspective.

The suspicion among evangelicals about the ecumenical movement, most noticeable in the more sectarian evangelical bodies but perceptible in mainline evangelicalism as well, tends to fasten ostensibly on the methods of the movement, its apparent concern with human contrivance rather than the unity already given by the Spirit. But in this, as in all other resistances to ecumenism, the fear of loss of distinctiveness also looms very large. The closer the contacts, the greater the agreement about goals, the more dangerous the threat to the very things which have given evangelicals their distinctive energy.

The possibility of ecumenically generated disunity within the Covenanting churches themselves was undoubtedly one of the factors which led to the failure of the proposals. One denomination, the Churches of Christ, paid the price of losing part of its membership during the course of the covenanting negotiations, when it took the preliminary step of uniting with the United Reformed Church. The same thing had happened earlier in the process of formation of the U.R.C.

Small churches, and churches which feel that they are at a social disadvantage, face particular problems about the exercise of power. There is an illuminating comment in a W.C.C. report on the racial dimension in ecumenism.

Many blacks feel that integration or merger causes fundamental and serious disruptions resulting in the elimination of leadership and the loss of black self-control, absorption and the loss of identity, accommodation and the loss of self-reliance.[8]

8 C. S. Song, 'Racism and the Unity of the Church' in *PCR Information* (1980), p. 50.

Unity, in other words, can increase the power of those who are already powerful, and threaten those whose contribution to the common pool could easily be submerged. The same impulses are at work at local church level in the hearts of those who wonder who will be churchwarden, or who will do the flowers, if their church unites with its more powerful next-door neighbour. It is not cynical or faithless to pay attention to such mixed motives and feelings, or to be aware of latent power struggles in what purports to be a spiritual movement. Like everything else, ecumenism has its unacceptable face. Sociological warnings about the perils of merger-mindedness, and the bureaucratic advantages of bigness and standardization, need to be taken seriously.

There are good grounds, therefore, for a certain over-all caution in trying to spell out ecumenical goals and evaluate ecumenical methods. Close contact with other Christian traditions can be enlarging and stimulating up to a point. But beyond that point the cost begins to look frighteningly high, nothing less than loss of identity. Reminders that the Christian faith is about death and resurrection, that loss of identity is the prelude to gaining a richer and fuller one, are not sufficient to quell the fear that any particular sacrifice may be needless, a faithless abandonment of the very things entrusted to a particular tradition for preservation. Death may be accepted with dignity, and in hope of resurrection, when it is seen to be inescapable. But ought it to be actively *sought*? May there not be a danger of gratuitous destructiveness unless every possible means has been attempted to preserve what is believed to be precious?

There is a further argument against any premature abandonment of distinctive identities in what has been said earlier on the subject of pluralism. In a pluralist society, the variety of church life can act as a kind of safety valve. Pluralism in the churches allows different identities to find religious expression in a way which is socially cohesive despite the formal divisions. Martin's analysis of the social consequences of monolithic and monopolistic Roman Catholicism,[9] serves as a warning against too ready acceptance of the goal of one totally united world-wide church. Monopolies tend to breed polarizations. A single church, unless it was conceived on lines very different from anything known in the past, might itself become a

9   Martin, *A General Theory of Secularization*, p. 63.

major factor in social conflict. This is already one of the elements in the Irish problem where the root fear on each side is of a monopoly by the other.[10] The fear is fed by the tendency of both religious traditions in Northern Ireland to identify with larger, more threatening, bodies outside themselves, on the one hand Britain, and on the other hand Southern Irish Roman Catholicism.

With all these warnings and discouragements along the ecumenical road, the question might well be asked, why go on? Why persist in tortuous negotiations and complex accommodations when the goal itself has so many ambiguous qualities, and the motives for pursuing it are so vulnerable to criticism?

Why indeed, unless in practice the movement is inspired and driven on by something more basic to Christian self-understanding than anything so far considered. It expresses itself in various ways. For Roman Catholics belief that the Church must be one is inseparable from belief in the Church itself. Richards puts it thus:

> A church that exists to direct men's eyes to limitless horizons, to refuse any attempt to introduce divisions, and consequent hostility, into human life, must necessarily be one and unique. Two churches could not do that job; they would simply introduce another cause of division. And that is what churches established on a national or a personal basis always do. The Catholic Church is the only one that cannot be identified with any particular nation or culture, historical period or theological and spiritual teacher.[11]

This is an interesting argument in that it combines the idea of unity with the idea of the church's transcendence of any particular time or place or culture. The sub-theme of the paragraph, namely that hostility should not be allowed to have a separate focus, is less convincing, and flies in the face of the warnings uttered by Martin. It is true that churches can contain a great deal of conflict within themselves, and ideally ought to be able to contain it all. But there may be other and better ways of containing conflict than by amalgamation into a single organization.

Outside the Roman Catholic tradition, the most powerful ecumenical language centres on the doctrine of reconciliation. This

10 ibid., p. 53.
11 Michael Richards, *The Church of Christ* (1983), quoted in the *Church Times*, 4 March 1983, p. 6.

encourages a more flexible and dynamic approach to the problems of disunity, in that the emphasis is on a theological method rather than on a clearly defined goal. The heart of the argument is that churches which exist to proclaim the Gospel that God has reconciled us to himself in Christ, undermine their own credibility if they remain unreconciled among themselves. And they undermine their effectiveness too, insofar as reconciliation between Christians is intended to be a foretaste of the reconciliation of the whole of humanity. This is why ecumenism is essential. But just as reconciliation between God and man opens up new and hitherto unsuspected depths of relationship, so reconciliation between Christians is a voyage of discovery. To specify in advance the form which unity must take for it to count as real reconciliation, is to forego the possibility of learning.

An imperative towards ecumenism, therefore, based on the doctrine of reconciliation, is both compelling and broad in its application; compelling because it is rooted in the heart of the Gospel; broad, because reconciliation is never a mere return to some supposed earlier state of harmony, but is nothing less than new creation.[12] And who can say what that will be until it happens?

There is, however, an even more compelling and broader motive for ecumenism – in the doctrine of God itself. It is here that what was said in chapter 4 about transcendence, and what is implied by Richards about the transcendence of the church, may possibly come together, and provide pointers to the way ahead.

Unity, in monotheistic traditions, is not thought of as a property of God which might conceivably have been different. For God to be God is for him to be one. Anything less than the One who created all things, who holds all things together, and will eventually bring all things into unity, is not God at all. This is the great lesson which Israel taught the world, and it lies at the root of all the claims to comprehensiveness and all the apparent imperialisms of Christianity, Islam and, at one remove, Marxism. Judaism itself, because it was based so firmly on blood relationship, had to contain this tremendous sense of oneness within its own peculiar sense of separate biological identity. But in Christianity with its universal vision, as in its later off-shoots, the search for unity in belief and fellowship, and ultimately for the unity of the human race, flows

12   2 Corinthians 5:17–19.

directly from belief in God. If this belief in the unity at the heart of all things is not somehow represented in the ways in which faith expresses itself and the structures in which it is embodied, then it is diminished and threatened. A universal faith in the reality which transcends all differences, has to be one.[13]

This is not to say that the actual road to unity is broad, obvious and easy. Quite the contrary. In a sinful and divided world a universal faith has to be protected if it is not to be eroded or corrupted by the degree of exposure to anything and everything which its comprehensiveness implies. And protection entails limitation. The God 'in whom we live and move and have our being', the God who is the ground and source of all other unities, has to be known in particular forms. Even the universal Word made flesh can only be communicated through the particular apprehensions of different human beings.

Thus arises the paradox of a universal faith necessarily expressed in practice through a variety of traditions. The making and breaking of such traditions, the movement into them and beyond them, the knowledge of them in their power and in their relativity, is the raw material of religious history and of the spiritual lives of individual believers. And it is this process, this double movement, which ecumenism at its most profound, attempts to represent.

I was recently involved in a discussion at which Cardinal Willebrands of the Vatican Secretariat for the Promotion of Christian Unity spoke informally about the need for Roman Catholics 'to relativize their feeling of uniqueness'.[14] It is a remarkable phrase, coming from that source, and links closely with a further, more conventional, comment about unity in Christ as a mystery rather than a matter of calculation. There in a nutshell are the three elements of ecumenical advance; the sense of uniqueness from which each participant starts; the acknowledgement of relativity; and the transcendent mystery to which such acknowledgement gives access.

It is because ecumenism is this kind of exercise, because ultimately and fundamentally it is about the character and quality of belief in God, that those who understand it in these terms press on despite the disappointments.

13 For an interesting development of the theme of this section see David Martin's *The Breaking of the Image* (1980), especially ch. 1.
14 An account of this meeting is to be found in *Rome 83: Returning the Pope's Visit* (1983).

An illustration may help to put some flesh on what has hitherto been a rather abstract exposition. It may at first sight seem a rather domestic illustration, a lapse from great and universal themes into the particular problems of the Church of England. However, the question of the internal unity of the Church of England, indeed Anglicanism in general, has wide repercussions. It is much more than a question of whether Anglican compromise is honest or dishonest, or the extent to which it is simply a product of special historical circumstances. It contains the possibility of discovering whether catholic and protestant traditions are truly reconcilable in ways which deepen the apprehension each has of God.

Searching exploration of this possibility in the English context is bedevilled by the tendency to think of traditions in terms of parties. What is badly needed, and what in some measure began to happen in the process of liturgical revision, is a meeting of minds on the basis of principles. Parties may be needed to safeguard principles, but the ARCIC discussions and the W.C.C. studies on Baptism, Eucharist and Ministry[15] have already demonstrated the gains to be found in moving beyond and beneath the sterile process of ecclesiastical labelling.

The catholic principle and the protestant principle are both rooted in the Gospel. The catholic principle rests on the certainty of God's promises. At its heart there is a sense of order. God has provided for us human beings fixed and definite ways in which we can relate to him. The sacraments, the priesthood, the church with its long history and its universal outreach, are all means through which God's promises to be with his people are made real and accessible. The vocabulary of catholicism contains words like 'safe', 'valid', 'authorized'. Threats to catholic order are resisted because they seem to put in jeopardy a whole structure of certainties on which the life of faith is based.

The protestant principle rests on the belief that the God who provides us with all these things is also able to dispense with them, precisely because he is God. In fact it goes further and asserts that at times they must be dispensed with, if only to make the point that it is God in his sovereignty and freedom with whom we have to do, rather than with some human construction. Typical protestant words are 'free', 'uncovenanted', 'faith'. Threats to protestant free-

15   *Baptism, Eucharist and Ministry*, W.C.C. (1982).

dom are resisted because they seem to impose human agencies between God and man.

In their actual application these broad principles interact and cut across party divisions. Catholics are not as wooden-headed as my previous paragraph might imply, nor are protestants so open. Catholics know that too much emphasis on 'order' is spiritually deadening, that the so-called 'certainties' can only be received by faith, and that if dependence on fixed and definite ways to God is taken to its logical conclusion, the end-product is not Christianity but superstition.

Likewise Protestants have long ago acknowledged that strict Protestantism is too bleak a faith to live by. If everything is put under question by the free sovereignty of God, if there are no fixed points where we can know that we are grasped and held by God, we are in the end reduced to the kind of dependence on ourselves whose logical conclusion is atheism.

Even the barest thumbnail sketch is enough to show how urgently each tradition needs the other, if they are to be saved from their own excesses. Though this is a negative reason for valuing diversity, it is not to be despised. On the pragmatic level the Church of England demonstrates again and again how within the context of a single church the sharp edges of extreme positions can usefully be smoothed away. This is the Anglican 'balance' so frequently commended in this book as a valuable first step in the reconciliation of apparent opposites. But my sketch of the catholic and protestant principles also indicates that this is not enough, indeed that this kind of smoothing away and concentration on reconciling different ways of doing things, may obscure a vital tension between different means of apprehending the mystery of God. The reconciliation of principles can thus lack depth, and in lacking depth miss an opportunity for real spiritual growth.

It is in the sharpness of contact between different churches and traditions that the most exciting things can happen. Despite the many deficiencies of bodies like the W.C.C., those close to them, and especially those who participate in major ecumenical events, know that they can be life-changing. This is why Anglican comprehensiveness, important though it is for demonstrating that Christians with very different viewpoints can live and work together in harmony, falls short as a model for ecumenism. Anglicans are tempted to rest on the unity they already enjoy, and to duck the hard theological questions. They thus fail to reap the fruits of real engagement with theological differences.[16]

If this is a valid criticism, and if as I have suggested earlier the real imperative for Christian unity is a theological one, it would seem that future patterns of ecumenism will need to place strong emphasis *both* on the real differences between traditions *and* on the way in which they can be transcended theologically, whether by returning to theological roots or by relativizing their uniqueness. This is not a recipe for a single united church, at least not in the foreseeable future. The problem of different Christian identities is much too pressing, and I suspect is the ultimate reason for the failure of many unity negotiations which had otherwise seemed on the brink of success. The only practicable way forward would seem to be to acknowledge a variety of Christian identities, to accept a degree of pluralism as inevitable, indeed desirable, and to try to contain it within an overall theological understanding which gives value to the differences, without encouraging a supermarket mentality.

Much ecumenical thinking is already moving in this direction. The importance attached to such concepts as 'dialogue',[17] 'conciliarity',[18] 'solidarity in conflict',[19] is evidence of a real desire to take the problem of identity seriously. However the ultimate ecumenical goal is defined, it is becoming clear that for the immediate future councils of churches in some appropriate form are going to have to provide the context within which these identities can relate to one another, and in which 'unity in diversity' becomes more than a convenient phrase to cover irreconcilable differences. The W.C.C. ideal of a 'conciliar fellowship of local churches'[20] has applications at many levels of organization.

In English the phrase 'conciliar unity' suffers from a certain ambiguity. It can refer to a unity in council between separate churches, or to the united council of a single church. It is therefore important to use it with some care. The ambiguity may have ad-

16 S. Sykes in *The Integrity of Anglicanism* (1978) elaborates this point at considerable length.
17 A word much used by Pope John Paul II.
18 See the W.C.C. Study Encounter SE/57: *Councils, Conciliarity and a Genuinely Universal Council* (1974).
19 This is an Eastern European phrase.
20 Formulated at the Nairobi Assembly (1975).

155

vantages, though, in inviting the thought that the distinction between the two meanings is not absolute. Might there not in fact be
many different degrees of conciliar fellowship? And if so, might not
the transition to a single conciliar church take place through a series
of very small steps within a conciliar body, rather than in a single
grand act of reunion? In the remainder of this chapter I intend to
explore some of the practical implications of this possibility, given
that the national context for it is provided by the British Council
of Churches. Since the failure of the covenanting proposals, this
with the Scottish, Welsh and Irish Councils remains as the sole
effective ecumenical agency in Britain.

To some people the idea that the B.C.C. should carry such
ecumenical weight is depressing in the extreme. It is a much criticized body, which suffers from chronic lack of funds, from dissipa-
tion of its inadequate resources in too many activities, and from the
unwillingness of member churches to entrust it with enough responsibility. In what follows I shall assume that these handicaps
can be removed, and that the superficial causes for complaint can
be effectively tackled. My concern is with the possibility of two
major developments which would transform the role of the Council,
and begin to mould it into the kind of instrument envisaged in the
last paragraph.

The first development has already started, and follows directly
from what has already been said about the importance of the theological framework within which churches relate. On the whole the
assumption within the B.C.C. has been that serious theological
discussion between churches takes place best in bilateral negotiations, and that the B.C.C. itself can therefore afford to be more
activist than reflective. The bias has expressed itself in agendas
crowded with quasi-political motions on a wide range of national
and international affairs, leaving little time for the discussion of
basic principles, or for probing the actual differences between
Christian perceptions. A new recognition of the need for a shift of
emphasis towards Faith and Order questions has been one of the
positive fruits of the demise of the Covenant. But the main hopes
for far-reaching change in this area rest on relationships with Rome.

A Roman Catholic decision to join the B.C.C. would alter the
balance dramatically, and provide the stimulus for all sorts of internal adjustments which are not likely to take place, without the
influx of some major new influence. In particular, Roman Catholic

insistence on proper theological understanding as the basis of all Christian action, and on agreement in the faith as the basis of all unity, would bring a new theological dimension into the Council's work. This would certainly not make the work any easier. Ecumenical theology encounters huge problems, not least that of maintaining integrity. One of the most insidious temptations in modern ecumenical circles, from which Rome itself is not exempt, is to bypass questions of biblical authority and to settle for high-sounding statements loaded with scriptural quotations, which hide an unacknowledged fundamentalism. But the stimulus from Rome to face such problems, and to wrestle with them in a context where there is already a conciliar commitment to one another, would be a great gain. It would also go a long way towards making the B.C.C. a more acceptable vehicle for the churches' main ecumenical hopes.

The second development I believe is necessary is likewise already present in embryo, but needs to be made much more explicit and robust. Unity in diversity, if it is to be genuine, seems to require the acceptance of some kind of principle of sufficiency. By this I mean the willingness of one church to accept the sufficiency of another church to do at least part of its task. The famous Lund principle stated that churches should not do separately what they might do together. A principle of sufficiency entails that churches should not do separately or together what one of their number can do on their behalf. This is an advance on the Lund principle in that it implies a high degree of trust and mutual acceptance. It also removes one of the main practical objections to ecumenism, namely the enormous waste of effort involved in duplicating or triplicating everything in order to ensure full ecumenical participation.

Take a simple example from a local ecumenical project. In the early days of an ecumenical relationship a disproportionate amount of time may have to be spent by the key people in the project in doing things together. Worship has to be conducted together, meetings chaired together, committee members carefully balanced, the equal partnership made clearly visible. But if a project develops well, high-profile ecumenism ceases to be so necessary. Members can simply concentrate on being Christian together, and do what each does best. They come to a state of trust in which each other's ministries and discipleship are accepted as sufficient. This is not to remove or ignore all differences. Different backgrounds, assumptions, theological perceptions, remain, but because they are brought

157

into the context of a common commitment, they cease to be barriers, and instead stimulate self-questioning and a common exploration of roots. No doubt the picture is idealized, but those who have worked at any depth in ecumenical circles know that something of this kind is possible.

And if locally, why not nationally? Why should national churches not operate a principle of sufficiency, allowing each church to do what it does best, without any suspicion of competition with the others?

In chapter 6 I have already indicated the advantages of such an arrangement in relation to establishment. There seems to be no inherent reason why, within a close ecumenical relationship, the Church of England's responsibilities towards the nation should not be acknowledged and welcomed as a service performed by that church, without others feeling the need to share it. At present, because it is confused with privilege, it tends to be a source of embarrassment, and can easily generate feelings of inferiority or superiority. Given sufficient trust and goodwill, however, most of the privileges can be shared, and what remains can be seen as the inevitable bundle of advantages and disadvantages which go with the exercise of this particular responsibility.

As part of the same package another church might provide a contrast to a nationally-orientated ministry, and adopt a much more critical stance towards the powers that be, by virtue of its very distance from them. In Britain in the nineteen-eighties the black-led churches, for instance, have things to say about the internal strains and inequalities in British society, which need to be heard as coming from the whole Christian community, but which cannot easily be said out of the kind of experience enjoyed by most members of the Church of England. Others churches have traditionally adopted radical social policies which feed through into the general thinking of the B.C.C., and create its image as being well to the left of centre. In this sense, if in no other, the Church of England needs the B.C.C., just as the B.C.C. needs the Church of England.

A principle of sufficiency could also have important pastoral consequences. It could ease the intolerable strain on some of the smaller churches in having to maintain a presence in areas where support is weak. I can think of a small Methodist congregation, for example, which receives hospitality and a ministry in Methodist style from the local parish priest. There is a genuine concern to preserve Methodist identity, but in this instance the Church of England is felt to be sufficient to provide it. In country areas the absurdity of separate clergy and ministers each having to cover huge areas has long been recognized. If, as suggested in the last chapter, Church of England parishes were to co-operate more closely in trying to ensure a more adequate coverage of different traditions, it ought not to be impossible to extend this ecumenically, at least in terms of pastoral care.

Practical schemes for sharing resources often founder on financial rocks. To move towards a greater degree of financial interdependence between churches would seem a very radical step indeed, but it is not impossible to make some small beginnings. My own diocese finances a number of posts in industrial mission, which are open to clergy of any denomination. In this particular instance we recognize the sufficiency of other ministries by appointing and paying the best man for the job, whatever his church. No doubt similar schemes operate elsewhere.

These are a few tiny examples which contain the seeds of future growth. It is worth remembering that it was the implicit acceptance of a principle of sufficiency which created the necessary conditions for the formation of the Church of South India. The missionary societies, by confining themselves to separate territories, had thereby committed themselves to the idea that in each area one church was sufficient. No such easy solution is possible in Britain. But small applications of the principle may pave the way for a wider recognition of its implications.

There are, however, two major obstacles against extending the idea much further. The first and most obvious is the question how and when it becomes appropriate to apply the principle of sufficiency to worship, and in particular to the eucharist. This is, of course, the question which has hitherto lain at the centre of unity negotiations, and I am fully conscious that it is not going to go away if it is merely approached from another angle. Nevertheless there comes a point at which a *de facto* unity achieved in some spheres, changes the terms in which theological and ecclesiological issues can be tackled. The fact that this particular obstacle remains, therefore, is not a reason for holding back in other spheres and on other occasions when the principle of sufficiency can be applied with integrity. In the present confused ecumenical situation, this is likely to mean different things in different places.

Consideration of the second major obstacle will take us forward into the next chapter. In a nutshell, it is a problem created by the concept of different Christian identities and complementary functions being held together in a context where there is real theological interchange and mutual acceptance. Given the complexity of this environment, how can the churches ever hope to speak with a united voice?

It is a problem which is already apparent in the B.C.C. Its internal machinery ensures that it says a great deal on a wide variety of topics, but all too often what it says fails to be 'owned' in any realistic way by its member churches. The danger facing all ecumenical bodies is that their voice becomes that of a small specialized group, and thus tends to be discounted by those who would listen much more attentively if they believed it was the authentic voice of widespread Christian opinion. I say this, not by way of criticism, since the problem is well known to those involved. Furthermore I am aware that the general approach advocated in this chapter might well make it worse.

But how far ought Christians expect to be able to agree on public issues? If theological differences have to be taken seriously as opening the way to a deeper apprehension of God, may not moral and social differences have to be taken equally seriously? And if so, may there not be a distinctive character of Christian witness, distinctive for holding together the three strands of social morality described at the end of chapter 3, rather than distinctive for giving simple answers to complex questions? The hugely difficult issue of nuclear weapons would seem to provide a suitable test case.

10

Nuclear Ethics

Despite its ambitious title this chapter has a very modest aim. It is intended to illustrate the Christian contribution to public thinking on a major contemporary issue by looking at some of the things theologians have said on the ethics of nuclear deterrence. There is no attempt to be comprehensive, nor to come to any conclusions on the issue itself. The main questions in view are; *How* do Christian thinkers tackle an issue of this kind? And is their contribution invalidated if it proves impossible to reach agreement?

In preparation for the World Council of Churches' International Hearing on Nuclear Weapons held in Amsterdam in November 1981, the planning committee gave much anxious thought to the business of arranging an appropriate theological input to the Hearing.[1] Should theologians be invited to speak first, thus setting out some general Christian guidelines within which subsequent reflection might take place? Or should they speak last, attempting to gather up what had been said in the rest of the Hearing, and subject it to a theological critique? Or should theological perceptions somehow be made to permeate the whole Hearing through the style of questioning, without there being any formal theological contribution at all? The issue was not merely organizational. Implied in it was an understanding of the nature of theology, interwoven with more mundane considerations about the way the Hearing was seen by the massive publicity machine which attended it.

In the end the need to make a firm opening Christian statement won the day, and four theologians spoke during the first main sitting. They were unanimous on the general issue of the immorality of nuclear war, as was the Hearing itself. Thereafter their assump-

---

1 A full account of the Hearing can be found in the W.C.C. publication *Before It's Too Late: The Challenge of Nuclear Disarmament* (1982).

tions, methods and detailed recommendations diverged widely from one another, and had little overt impact on the remainder of the proceedings. The fact that their attitudes strongly reflected the contexts from which they came, implies no discredit on them as theologians; any worthwhile theology must speak to those to whom it is addressed. But as frequently happens at ecumenical events, to hear these four addresses one after the other was a vivid reminder of the extent to which all theology belongs to a particular time and place, and needs the stimulus of minds from other cultures if it is to transcend its origins.

Roger Shinn, speaking out of an American context, clearly showed the agony of a man conscious of his nation's immense responsibility. He was both attracted and repelled by nuclear deterrence. As a Christian he could offer only a willingness to go on wrestling with intractable political problems without sinking into fatalism or despair. Christianity, in his testimony, was seen as a source of idealism and hope, not a basis for specific moral guidance.

Burgess Carr, a liberation theologian from Liberia, tried to set the whole problem within the context of Third World concerns, and concentrated his attack on the immorality of the arms race as a major example of international exploitation and waste. He also asked some pointed questions about the role of the State in the purpose of God, whether it is to be seen as an end in itself or as an instrument for mediating justice to the world's poor.

Edward Schillebeeckx endorsed the views of the Dutch anti-nuclear movement and, surprisingly for a Roman Catholic theologian, totally rejected Just War theory on the grounds that it was a relic of feudalism. His theology was the most subtle of the four, maintaining a careful balance between fallible political decisions and the ultimate dimension, the expansion of the horizon of moral responsibility, within which such decisions have to be made. Immediate political goals in disarmament, for instance, need a vision of ultimate peace which allows those who share the vision to take political risks. He also spoke about the importance of negative painful experiences, in stimulating the protesting conscience to action. In a later session of the Hearing another Dutch Christian spokesman elaborated on this protesting mentality as found in the Netherlands, and related it to the experience of being a small country.[2]

2   ibid., pp. 356–7.

Günter Krusche from East Germany focussed his concern on confidence-building as the most effective practical means of preventing war. His contribution illustrated the constraints within which churches have to operate in socialist societies, but there was also an undercurrent of theological protest which surfaced in discussion of the Lutheran *Status Confessionis*. At some point, according to this way of thinking, the church has to make a confessing stand, the Christian conscience has to say 'so far and no further'. In the meantime Christians have to talk and explore the possibilities of peace with all who show any concern for it, whatever their political label.

All four theologians spent more of their time defending practical policies than in trying to elaborate some coherent Christian framework within which actual decisions might be made. Such theology as emerged was fragmentary, and consisted more of individual Christian 'insights' related to particular circumstances than the general guidelines which, perhaps naively, had been hoped for. The Hearing Group thus found itself on shifting sands when it turned to its task of attempting some Christian response to what it had heard. In the end the main ethical substance of its report was based on Just War theory, though the title was not used explicitly. The motive for reverting to the theory was the sheer absence of any alternative framework for trying to evaluate the evidence as a whole. Remove Just War theory and what is left is either straightforward pacifism, honourable in itself, but not a political option for most of the nations involved in the Hearing, or a series of *ad hoc* marginal comments from different Christian perspectives.

I have told this story at some length, partly because I was personally involved in it, and partly as a warning against supposing that there is any easy way of bringing theological understanding to bear on a subject with so many complex ramifications, and so heavily dependent on a constantly changing analysis of the relevant facts. The same point is made in *The Church and the Bomb*, though it was frequently overlooked in the public reactions to the book.

Except in the most general sense there are no timeless moral conclusions of Christian ethics in regard to nuclear weapons. Indeed, the conclusions of Christian thinkers writing only a generation ago on nuclear weapons can only be of indirect value for us today, for the simple reason that the facts which we address are significantly different from those known to them.[3]

Despite this warning, however, a good deal of weight can be placed on general conclusions drawn from Just War theory, as it was in the W.C.C. Report, in *The Church and the Bomb* itself, in the recent pastoral letter of the U.S. Roman Catholic bishops,[4] and in numerous other writings.

The argument in a nutshell is that nuclear weapons offend Just War criteria on two grounds. First, on account of their size and the character of nuclear explosions, they are bound to be indiscriminate in their effects; secondly, their extreme and long-lasting destructiveness must be disproportionate to any reasonable war aim. These two characteristics put them in a different category from conventional weapons, render them morally unacceptable, and make it wrong even to possess and intend to use them, let alone actually fight with them.

It is a strong argument, set out especially well by the Roman Catholic bishops, and has convinced many. There are, however, three weak links in the chain of reasoning, which have been the focus of much discussion. The claim that there is a basic qualitative difference between nuclear and conventional weapons has been questioned by some on the grounds that very small nuclear weapons are now scarcely distinguishable from very large conventional ones. While there is clearly a huge difference between all-out nuclear war and a minor conventional exchange, there is no sudden qualitative leap in passing from one type of weapon to another.

If this first weak link is strengthened by introducing the idea of a psychological nuclear threshold, then a second weakness appears. The argument at this stage depends on the assumption that to cross the nuclear threshold using even the smallest weapon would create an overwhelming risk of greater and greater nuclear escalation. It is a highly plausible assumption, but its weakness in what purports to be an abstract moral argument is that it rests on strategic and political judgements about the likely course of events. The main moral claim therefore begins to take on a much more problematic and political character.

The third weak link concerns the moral relationship between the

3 *The Church and the Bomb: Nuclear Weapons and Christian Conscience* (1982).
4 *The Challenge of Peace: God's Promise and Our Response* (1983).

actual use of nuclear weapons and the expressed intention to use them. Much of the discussion around this point is confused by ambiguities in the concept of intention.[5] In different contexts, for example, it can be used to mean 'overall purpose' or 'preparedness' or 'willingness'. When advocates of nuclear deterrence argue that the intention of possessing weapons is to deter attack, the word is being used in the first sense. When critics point to the close practical connection between intention and use, the evidence usually cited is evidence of preparedness. When a radical distinction is made between the morality of deterrence before it breaks down, and the new moral situation created by its failure, the implication is that the actual willingness to use nuclear weapons might be very different in the two different circumstances.[6] This element of ambiguity may not invalidate the simple case that intention and use are morally equivalent, but it undoubtedly weakens it.

The radical case against nuclear weapons based solely on Just War principles is thus not invulnerable. But even if it were, would it be enough? What kind of weight ought general abstract arguments about moral principles to carry in the actual business of political decision-making? Here we enter a different realm of discussion, a realm touched on in chapter 3. How do moral principles relate to the realities of political power and responsibility? Ought the churches to try to make specific political judgements, or ought they to rest content with moral generalities? There are those who say that day-to-day politics cannot be conducted on the basis of moral principles at all; the principles need to be there, well in the background, but the choices in practice depend almost wholly on circumstances.

Stuart Hampshire favours political instinct. Well-trained instincts can grasp more features of a complex situation than abstract analysis. Abstract morality 'places a prepared grid upon conduct . . . and thereafter only tends to see the pieces as they are divided by the lines on the grid'.[7] Politicians who fly by the seat of their pants are likely to do better than those who stick rigidly to hard and fast principles. Dorothy Emmet with her warning about choosing only one colour of light from the moral prism, is making basically the

5 There is an excellent discussion of 'intention' in G. Goodwin (ed.), *Ethics and Nuclear Deterrence* (1982), especially chapters 4 and 5.
6 Richard Harries (ed.), *What Hope in an Armed World?* (1982), p. 100.
7 Hampshire (ed.), *Public and Private Morality*, p. 40.

same point.[8] So are those who see choices of this kind as essentially choices between evils.[9]

Yet principles matter. There is a famous passage in which Weber sets out the relationship between what he calls 'an ethic of responsibility' and 'an ethic of ultimate ends'. Any moral approach to politics must somehow weave together these two which, under various titles, represent the two major strands in all ethical theory; Utilitarianism and Kantianism are their classic forms. Weber describes those who too easily parade their ultimate ends and 'pass the watchword, "The world is stupid and base, Not I".' He goes on:

> I would first inquire into the degree of inner poise backing this ethic of ultimate ends. I am under the impression that in nine cases out of ten I deal with windbags who do not fully realize what they take upon themselves but who intoxicate themselves with romantic sensations. From a human point of view this is not very interesting to me, nor does it move me profoundly. However, it is immensely moving when a *mature* man – no matter whether old or young in years – is aware of a responsibility for the consequences of his conduct and really feels such responsibility with heart and soul. He then acts by following an ethic of responsibility and somewhere he reaches the point where he says: 'Here I stand; I can do no other.' That is something genuinely human and moving. And every one of us who is not spiritually dead must realize the possibility of finding himself at some time in that position. In so far as this is true, an ethic of ultimate ends and an ethic of responsibility are not absolute contrasts but rather supplements, which only in unison constitute a genuine man . . .[10]

The Lutheran echoes bring us close to what was said by Krusche about *Status Confessionis* in circumstances where adherence to principle can be very costly indeed.[11] Schillebeeckx, too, accepts the ambiguities of all actual political decision-making, yet recognizes an appropriate 'foolishness' which Christian concern with ultimacy brings into the political discussion.

8   See p. 74.
9   Harries, p. 107.
10 Weber, *Essays in Sociology*, p. 126.
11 W.C.C., *Before It's Too Late*, p. 97.

The churches should not pretend any kind of ethical superiority; they share the uncertainties of our so-called 'culture'. In spite of this they will have no choice but to speak out in all humility but from within a fundamental, prophetic ethical indignation.[12]

The Pope has spoken of 'audacious gestures of peace', while at the same time refusing to condemn reliance on nuclear deterrence as long as the general movement is in the direction of disarmament.[13] Emmet's emphasis on generosity and liberty of spirit as the special religious contribution to social morality, which has nevertheless somehow to be woven in with the other strands of social cohesion and rational prudential decision-making, fits into the same pattern.[14] Social morality must never be so ordered as to deny scope for religious vision, nor so visionary as to leave the stage to Weber's irresponsible windbags. But where does one draw the line? There is in fact no general way of deciding precisely how an ethic of responsibility and an ethic of ultimate ends meet and mix with one another, and this is why Christians are likely to remain divided on great issues, unless the principles at stake are so blindingly clear that there is no real scope for disagreement.

I have suggested that on the subject of nuclear weapons the principles are not as clear as some would like them to be. Dunstan goes further and claims that there is no specific 'Christian approach' to such questions at all, just as 'there is no specifically "Christian" way of waging war, or of amputating limbs, or of fixing oil prices, or of deciding for or against the nuclear generation of energy'.[15] Reliance on Just War theory merely substantiates the point, since the theory was not derived from Christian tradition but from Greece and Rome, whence the medieval canonists dressed it up in Christian language. For Dunstan the prime Christian responsibility in tackling problems of this kind is to bring Christian minds to bear on the business of politics 'working within the terms and categories given them by politics itself'.[16] Christian theology enables the handling of contradictions, it entails a widening of horizons, a refusal to 'simplify, reduce or become partisan'. The Christian doctrine of man as both sinful and redeemed makes it possible

12 ibid., p. 87.
13 Pope John-Paul II, *World Peace Day Message* (1979).
14 See p. 64.
15 Goodwin, p. 40.
16 ibid., p. 45.

to walk between a facile optimism – a belief that all things are possible to us once we have perfected the systems, whether it be a weapons system or an instrument for world government – and a numbing despair, the assumption that the worst must happen, so that there is nothing we can do about it.[17]

What is interesting about Dunstan's approach is the implied assumption that the Christian input to the discussion of nuclear ethics is first and foremost a theological one. In fact it is possible to generalize the point and say that the prime Christian contribution to social ethics is in the indicative rather than in the imperative mood.[18] In terms of the principles by which people should live and societies order themselves, Christians have little to say that could not be said by any reasonable person of goodwill. It is Christian belief about the kind of place the world is, about the depth of human sinfulness and the possibilities of divine grace, about judgement and hope, incarnation and salvation, God's concern for all and his care for each, about human freedom and divine purpose – it is beliefs such as these which make the difference, and provide the context within which the intractable realities of social and political life can be tackled with wisdom and integrity.

Within such an understanding of the Christian task the actual differences between Christian ethical judgements need not matter so greatly. Indeed where there are differences they can act as a valuable warning against the kind of moral absolutism which politicians are as much tempted to subscribe to as anyone else who is bewildered by the complexities of modern life. In chapter 7 I referred to the importance of the distinctive *quality* of the debate on public issues which the churches might be able to offer, rather than a distinctive set of 'Christian policies'. This may seem an unglamorous role. In many ways it is much more satisfying to be able to parade moral certainties, and within the total Christian community there will always be those who, rightly and properly, do so. There will also be times and circumstances when, as my discussion of Weber has suggested, Christian consciences will be able to unite around some great moral issue with a unanimity which gives the judgement unique authority. The condemnation of racism, for in-

17 ibid., p. 47–8.
18 Habgood, *A Working Faith*, p. 114.

stance, has almost achieved that kind of status. But the occasions are likely to be rare.

In the W.C.C. Report on nuclear weapons a tentative parallel was drawn between nuclear and racist policies.[19] In very general terms the parallel could be said to hold. Few, if any, Christians or few sane people of any kind, for that matter, would wish to give moral legitimacy to nuclear war-fighting. But to move from this general condemnation through the intricacies of particular nuclear policies and the moral subtleties of some of the best thinking on deterrence, is to take a very long journey indeed. And at the end of it, agreement is much less certain. Those who have a clear vision of what ought to be done, lament Christian divisiveness and see it as a weakness. Those who see no easy answers, may have cause to be grateful that a mature Christianity can contain these differences, and thus help to prevent the political debate polarizing into sterile confrontation. As Alan Booth has suggested, and it is a suggestion which has a much wider application than in this particular internal debate, it is the task of men of moral earnestness 'to deflate the moral pretensions of nations as a contribution to peace'.[20]

I end this very brief discussion of a huge subject with a few thoughts on civil disobedience. They arise directly out of what has gone before because, if there is any large-scale civil disobedience in Britain in the immediate future, it is likely to be linked in the first instance with the issue of nuclear weapons. Early in 1983 the British Council of Churches produced a working paper entitled *Civil Disobedience as Christian Obedience: Theological Reflections on Non-Violent Direct Action in relation to the Nuclear Issue*[21]. This is fairly modest in its actual recommendations – mainly to 'study the matter carefully' – which were endorsed by the Assembly, but the underlying implication is that the nuclear issue is one on which Christians could and should take sides and, if not press their point directly, at least give support and assistance to those who in conscience feel bound to do so.

The general point that there are extreme circumstances in which the rights of conscience against the State must be upheld even at the cost of breaking the law, can be conceded at once. There is a

19 W.C.C., *Before It's Too Late*, p. 30.
20 Quoted in Wilkinson, *The Church of England and the First World War*, p. 209.
21 Unpublished B.C.C. paper.

long and honourable history of religious defiance of unjust regimes. But how extreme is 'extreme'? And how does the fact that a democracy may provide many alternative legitimate means for expressing dissent, affect the moral implications of illegal action?

If, as I have argued, there is only the most general Christian agreement on the subject of nuclear weapons, and if disagreements about particular policies can be accepted as a potential source of strength rather than a weakness, then it seems to me that the circumstances of the present nuclear debate in Britain are not so extreme as to justify an official Christian endorsement of law-breaking. The nation, Christians included, is divided on a matter of political judgement, not on a clear-cut issue of right and wrong. And the appropriate way to settle a matter of political judgement is the normal democratic one.

None of what I have said denies the right of individuals to follow their conscience, and if this leads them into law-breaking, to suffer the consequences. But I cannot endorse the view that there is any Christian obligation to support them.

The problem about civil disobedience is that although it may begin with very limited aims, it tends to feed upon itself. The excitement and the publicity generated by it, and the unreal expectations aroused by it, push it into more and more extreme forms of confrontation. It unleashes forces which are difficult to control. Weber again, has some wise words:

> In the world of realities, as a rule, we encounter the ever-renewed experience that the adherent of an ethic of ultimate ends suddenly turns into a chiliastic prophet. Those, for example, who have just preached 'love against violence' now call for the use of force for the *last* violent deed, which would then lead to a state of affairs in which *all* violence is annihilated . . . The proponent of an ethic of absolute ends cannot stand up under the ethical irrationality of the world.[22]

The genie of disobedience finds too much to its liking in an imperfect world to go back easily into the bottle. Britain, in particular, with its reliance on social conventions rather than constitutional rights, is especially vulnerable to civil disobedience, and could lose much of what is admirable about the British way of doing

22 Weber, *Essays in Sociology*, p. 121.

things if it were to become widespread. The alternative is to go on trying to contain protest movements, demonstrations and other such activities within agreed procedures, recognizing that this may need more tolerance on both sides, and a greater willingness actually to talk to one another, than has hitherto been apparent.

If, as may happen, confrontations become sharper, Christians who differ from one another may suffer the humiliation of discovering, as in Northern Ireland, that political differences are more important to them than brotherhood in Christ. In such circumstances the gospel of forgiveness as the ultimate basis of all true peace, takes on a fresh urgency.

11

Where Do We Go From Here?

'I should see the garden far better', said Alice to herself, 'if I could get to the top of that hill: and here's a path that leads straight to it – at least, no, it doesn't do that –' (after going a few yards along the path and turning several sharp corners), 'but I suppose it will at last. But how curiously it twists! It's more like a corkscrew than a path! Well, *this* turn goes up the hill, I suppose – no, it doesn't! This goes straight back to the house! Well then, I'll try it the other way.'

And so she did: wandering up and down, and trying turn after turn, but always coming back to the house, do what she would. Indeed, once, when she turned a corner rather more quickly than usual, she ran against it before she could stop herself.[1]

As Alice was soon to discover, her frustrations in Looking-Glass land were the frustrations of pursuing a mirror-image. Mirrors show us where we are. If we want to go somewhere else, we may have to walk in the opposite direction.

So far in this book I have been trying to look at the church scene in Britain, and at the Church of England in particular, with the use of a sociological mirror. The picture which has emerged, and the modest recommendations made along the way, have been mostly conservative. This ought not to be surprising. The more closely one looks at what one is, and the more conscious one is of the constraints and influences of one's environment, the less likely one is to succeed in going somewhere radically different. The path leads back to the house where one is already. In this sense the exercise of looking in a mirror is itself a conservative one. And when it goes on to reveal, as in the case of the churches, a delicate system of checks and balances, of stabilizing and destabilizing forces within a highly

1 Lewis Carroll, *Through the Looking-Glass*, Chapter 2.

172

complex reality, the pressures towards maintaining the *status quo* are very strong indeed.

This may seem paradoxical in that sociologists have a well-earned reputation for being fomenters of revolution. Their discipline certainly enables them to ask sharp questions and to disclose unsuspected and unsettling connections. But sharp questions and awkward revelations do not necessarily lead to radicalism. They can equally well have the effect of freezing those at whom they are directed in postures which have hitherto felt secure. Unwelcome probings can merely strengthen the conviction of those being probed that worldly wisdom leads inevitably to ungodliness. Analysis can also reveal strengths as well as weaknesses, and show the alternatives as so unattractive that even those who are conscious of the need for change, decide to stay where they are. Conservatism, in fact comes in many shapes and sizes. There can be a dishonest conservatism which tries to hide itself away from uncomfortable realities. There can be a supine conservatism which cannot summon up the energy to change. But there can also be a faithful conservatism based on a right and proper appreciation of what one has already.

In asking, therefore, whether the basically conservative conclusions to which this book has come are justified in the circumstances or not, it is important to judge whether the conclusions result from the method, or from timidity, or whether they are based on a realistic appraisal of the facts.

The method, as we have already seen, has been one-sided. Alice discovered that she could only make progress by walking away from her own image in a manner which at first seemed foolish. Much Christian experience points in the same direction. Analysis is not enough. There has to be a vision and motive for acting in ways which transcend our situation, and it has to come from something outside the analysis itself.

At this point we enter familiar Christian territory, and the 'something else' which is needed begins to assume the dimensions of another book for its description. 'Stop looking at yourself and look to Christ' is the simple and obvious formula. Christianity is not primarily about *us*, but about what God has given us. It is faithless to concentrate on the extent to which churches are conditioned by society, while neglecting the transforming power of the Gospel.

Sociology is not the only mirror held up for us. The true image of man is to be found in the face of Jesus.

Against the background of such straightforward Christian conviction, tortuous sociological arguments and the 'nicely calculated less or more' can seem perverse. Yet the contrast between sociological analysis and theological assertion is not quite as stark as the last paragraph might imply. The difficulty is that theology can be analysed by sociologists no less than sociology can be challenged by theologians. Gill's books are an attempt to do just this.[2] But the awareness of theological limitations is much older, and dates at least from the days when Biblical scholars in their quest for the historical Jesus were accused of looking down a well and seeing the reflections of their own faces.[3] Nowadays there are a multitude of theologies, from those which claim to be comprehensive to others, like 'black theology' or 'liberation theology', which are quite explicitly related to the social circumstances of their origin. Nor is there any return from such theological complexity to some simple biblical religion which precedes theological reflection. The Bible itself belongs within a particular society which both shaped it and was shaped by it. The Christ we look to is inevitably the Christ *we* look to.

Of course there are degrees of bondage to social bias. There is all the difference in the world between using Christianity to confirm one's own prejudices, and studying it with all the help available and responding to it with all the openness one can. I am in no sense endorsing social determinism. It is one of the great characteristics of living Christian faith that it constantly breaks through the fragile shell which human societies create to contain it. Whatever the social constraints, human beings can still be brought, maybe by twisting roads and with many false turns, face to face with God. But, as I have argued in chapter 4, to be aware of *some* social bias and to admit the validity of differing perceptions of God, are important conditions for knowing him more fully as transcendent. To this extent sociological analysis, far from being a challenge to faith, can actually be an ally. It drives faith to look more deeply at its own roots. 'Now we see through a glass darkly. . . .' Face-to-face knowledge belongs properly to the end of time.

2 Robin Gill, *The Social Context of Theology* and *Theology and Social Structure.*
3 This is the summary of Albert Schweitzer's monumental *The Quest of the Historical Jesus* (1906).

Though the method of this study has been one-sided, therefore, I do not believe there is any simple alternative which can bypass the need for some such analysis. It is by bringing together a whole variety of perceptions, by listening to Christians in different traditions, by allowing interplay between analysis and conviction, by interpreting experience in the light of Christian tradition, and Christian tradition in the light of experience, that we begin to be rescued from some of our distortions and see the way ahead more clearly. It has been a major theme of this book that in a pluralist society there is no honest means of escaping from pluralism into some impregnable absolutism. Pluralism can remind us, however, of how much we need each other. And in that acceptance of one another in our differences lies the possibility of a more complete obedience.

Daniel Jenkins makes the point that old churches are not very good at innovation. This is a potentially dangerous statement because 'churches are very conservative institutions and . . . are always glad to find excuses for maintaining familiar routines and avoiding the dislocation and difficulty of doing anything new'.[4]

This is the temptation to timidity, mentioned earlier. But there is also the temptation to try to be something one is not, to dress mutton as lamb, and to forfeit the real strengths of continuity and experience and long-acknowledged responsibilities. I suggested in chapter 9 that in an ideal ecumenical environment churches should be able to do what each does best, without pride or competitiveness, yet able to learn from one another, and correct one another, and together move towards a greater Christian wholeness.

It is against this kind of background that the particular strengths of the Church of England, and its underlying conservatism, could be rescued from their defects. Then instead of feeling guilty about being old, and hard to change, and stuck in tradition, and overstretched in relation to its historic responsibilities, the church might begin to regain fresh confidence in what it is and could be within the purposes of God. As long as it thinks of itself in exclusive terms, the reasons for guilt remain. But within a wider Christian community, where guardianship of the Christian heritage and radical reappraisal of it are allowed to interact, and where both are seen as the stimulus the other needs to deepen its roots in God, there is no

4   Jenkins, *The British*, p. 177.

need to feel guilty about treasuring one's own traditions and fulfilling one's special responsibilities. Indeed the restoration of confidence in what God has led us to become, and the challenge to it through interaction with others, are part of the process of restoring that confidence in God himself, which is so essential for today's Christians.

In an age when so much is open to criticism and subject to change, a well-informed and responsive traditionalism has a vital role to play. As in the famous parable of the life-boat being repaired at sea, the attempt to tackle all problems at once, to remove all rotting planks simultaneously, is a recipe for disaster.[5] But those temperamentally inclined to grasp conservative solutions need to know *why* they are being conservative on some issue, and what its limits are. My defence of establishment, for instance, was based fundamentally on an assessment of the needs of the nation, and a view of the church as not confined to those whose religious commitment is most explicit and most ready to express itself in overt religious activity. Both assessments depend on circumstances, and as an establishment-minded Anglican I acknowledge my need of those whose assessments are different and who will make sure that, should circumstances change radically, the Church of England is not allowed to slide away from the prospect of being disestablished. There are no absolutes in these matters. Neither is there any virtue in changing course every time the wind blows from a different direction.

An American Jesuit, writing in a very different context, has some wise words about the proper conservatism of bishops.

Bishops should be conservative, in the best sense of that word. They should not endorse every fad, or even every theological theory. They should 'conserve', but to do so in a way that fosters faith, they must be vulnerably open and deeply involved in a process of creative and critical absorption. In some, perhaps increasingly many instances, they must take risks, the risks of being tentative or even quite uncertain and above all reliant on others in a complex world. Such a process of clarification and settling takes time, patience, and courage. Its greatest enemy is

5   See Martin, *The Breaking of the Image*, p. 155.

ideology, the comfort of being clear, and above all the posture of pure defence of received formulations.[6]

These words could well act as a summary of much of what I have tried to say about churches as whole. They are especially applicable to bishops, because bishops have a peculiarly difficult task in getting the balance right. They have to combine a leadership role (carrying the implication that it ought in some sense to be 'prophetic') with a conservationist role (as guardians of the church's unity and continuity). Hence many episcopal dilemmas; and hence the quotation from David Martin with which this book began: 'A bishop should "speak out", but what can he say?'

Those who speak out must either speak in platitudes or run the risk of dividing their flocks. Those who fail to speak out lead their flocks from behind.

There is, however, a third option, already hinted at in chapter 3, which takes seriously the different gifts of different groups and individuals within the churches and which, in line with what was said in the last chapter, does not suppose that the church can or must speak with a single voice, whether episcopal or not. The important thing, according to this option, is for church leaders to create the kind of environment within which prophetic voices can be heard. This means giving space and encouragement to those who actually know about the matter in hand, and can speak out of their own direct experience.

It is a fact that much of the new life in the churches arises, not from the top, but from individuals and groups and those with some special interest, who catch a vision and pursue it and eventually manage to share it. Top-heavy initiatives, on the other hand, often cause resentment and resistance, especially when they drive too obviously from the supposed need felt by leaders to be seen to 'do something'.

A wise conservatism, far from frustrating local ideas and initiatives, can positively help in the creation of an environment which encourages them. Basic to risk-taking is the need for an underlying confidence. A church which generates confidence, therefore, ought at the same time to be generating new life, including prophetic criticism. Over-confidence, the confidence of those who are so convinced of their own rightness that they have no eyes or ears for

6 R. A. McCormick, *How Brave a New World?* (1981), p. 258–9.

anything else, kills it. But there is a quiet kind of confidence within which it becomes possible to listen to hitherto unheard, and maybe discordant, voices. And that is the confidence of those who value, respect, and live by their tradition without absolutizing it in a way which makes them vulnerable to every new thing which might threaten it.

My hope is that the analysis I have attempted in this book may itself be a source of such quiet confidence. Nobody can pretend that the state of the churches in present-day Britain gives much comfort to Christian believers. Traditional institutional religion is going through a bad time. But equally nobody can pretend that there is not a vital role in our society which the Christian faith can and must fulfil. The important thing is to face the problems honestly enough so that a mature Christian faith can be brought to bear on them, to work together openly enough so that different Christian traditions can make up one another's deficiencies, and to look beyond the complexities of present experience faithfully enough to keep alive the vision of God.

Appendix: Theological Reflections on Compromise

All Government, indeed every human benefit and enjoyment, every virtue, and every prudent act, is founded on compromise and barter.

Edmund Burke on American Independence

The reason that the right will continue to run away is partly that they have been running away for so long that it has become a habit, and partly that the flight to ignominy always consists of single steps; they are never asked to do anything that is more than an extension, and usually only a small extension, of something they have already done.

Bernard Levin (on the right wing of the British Labour Party)

If compromise is a major part of the art of politics, at what point should a politician stop compromising? When does the negative element in any compromise, the concessions and surrenders it implies, outweigh or undermine the positive value of the agreements or promises achieved through it? Are those who wave the banner of 'No compromise', and who stress the pejorative meaning of the word, the only true leaders and prophets, or are they merely being foolishly unrealistic?

Politicians live constantly with such questions and learn, more or less successfully, to keep upright on the slippery ground between statesmanlike compromise and unprincipled surrender. It is not often that they look to theologians for support because there is a strong suspicion, whether justified or not, that theology already leans too far in the direction of absolutism for political comfort. Religious people seem to give the impression that there is something vaguely disreputable about compromise. This essay is an attempt to redress the balance, to indicate that there are elements within

179

the Christian tradition which may be of greater usefulness to them than many practical politicians suppose.

A recent cartoon showed Moses receiving the Ten Commandments on Mount Sinai, and saying to God, 'I think they would go over better if we called them voluntary guide-lines.' The joke does its work at a number of levels; in part pointing the finger at contemporary Christians for loss of faith in absolute standards; in part acknowledging the sheer difficulty in actually applying such standards in the real world. It is an old moral dilemma. An apparently straightforward command, 'Thou shalt not kill', has been interpreted and qualified and restricted in its application since the first day it was uttered. The Israelites had no compunction about killing their enemies or executing wrongdoers. They knew the difference between justifiable and unjustifiable homicide. Their massive elaborations of the law represented increasingly sophisticated attempts to uphold its inviolability while making it workable in practice.

Christian casuistry followed the same pattern. The more rigorous their beliefs about moral obligation, the more elaborate were the various expedients which practical moralists had to adopt in order to make life tolerable. The interpretation of the so-called 'strenuous commands' in the Sermon on the Mount have always been a crux of Christian ethics. Those who have felt themselves impelled to 'give to those who ask' and 'turn the other cheek', literally and without any qualification, have almost always had to live their lives in some separated and specialized community, which by its very existence offers a measure of protection against the full force of the standards it professes.

The uneasy conscience of many good Christians about their failure to live up to the demands of the Gospel has its roots in the awareness that there is something hard and uncompromising at the heart of their faith, to which extreme moral reactions bear witness. The rich young ruler of Luke 18:18–23 was good by any ordinary standard, yet still felt his need of something more. Nor is it just particular stories, sayings or demands which create this unease. Religion itself, in any but its most complacent forms, has a tendency towards absolutism through the very nature of the claims made about God. Religious language is the language of extremes, because somehow it has to attain enough velocity to secure lift-off. The transition from earth-borne language to language about God has to be signalled by words which express a sense of finality and all-inclusiveness.

Consider the famous passage in Colossians where Paul's words about Christ take wings:

> He is the image of the invisible God; his is the primacy over all created things. In him everything in heaven and on earth was created, not only things visible but also the invisible orders of thrones, sovereignties, authorities and powers; the whole universe has been created through him and for him. And he exists before everything, and all things are held together in him. He is, moreover, the head of the body, the church. He is its origin, the first to return from the dead, to be in all things alone supreme. For in him the complete being of God, by God's own choice, came to dwell. Through him God chose to reconcile the whole universe to himself, making peace through the shedding of his blood upon the cross – to reconcile all things, whether on earth or in heaven, through him alone.[1]

Note the repeated use of words like 'all', 'every', 'complete' with the imagery of all-inclusiveness, balanced by equally decisive language at the opposite pole – the word 'alone'. Such language has echoes all the way through the Bible, and sets the tone for the believer's own life. In the previous paragraph Paul prays that his readers 'may receive from him [God] *all* wisdom and spiritual understanding for *full* insight into his will, so that your manner of life may be worthy of the Lord and *entirely* pleasing to him'.[2] The exaggerations, if that is what it is right to call them, like the use of hyperbole in the teaching of Jesus, are not mere exaggerations. They have a very definite religious function. But they carry with them the danger that this function will be misunderstood, and the believer will find himself trapped by an impossible set of ideals and demands. To lessen the demand of the imperatives is to weaken the sense that the believer is confronted by nothing less than God himself. To accept them at their face value is to lose one's hold on ordinary human existence.

A strange book by Nigel Balchin, published in 1947, expressed on behalf of some of those who had lived through the thirties and

1 Colossians 1:15–20 (N.E.B.).
2 Colossians 1:9–10 (N.E.B.).

forties, their sense of disillusionment with the exaggerated certainties of those who thought they knew where they were going. Entitled *Lord I Was Afraid*, it was a defence of the servant in the parable who hid his talent in the ground because he could not see any clear way of using it with integrity. In the final scene of the book, the hero is drowning in a latter-day flood and complains to Methuselah:

> We stood at the cross-road of time, with all the signposts down. We saw error and ignorance and prejudice and stupidity go marching boldly down the roads away from somewhere and towards anywhere. The bands were playing and the flags flying. It would have been easy to follow. But we stood there, fumbling for our lost compass and our missing map – waiting for the stars to come out and give us a bearing; waiting until it was light; and in the end waiting because we had always waited. That was our failure. And we must drown for it. Yes, yes, we know. We have no complaint, and ask no mercy. It is for God to decide what sort of man he wants, and he has always had a partiality for the stone-slinging, ruddy-faced sinner who could slay you his ten thousands, and come straight home to a bout of hearty adultery, and then weep in his bed in repentance. But Michal, Saul's daughter, despised him in her heart, and so do we. We have slain no Goliaths, but Uriah's blood is not on our hands . . .[3]

If David, with his extremes and his excesses, is the archetypal believer, then Balchin's hero can stand for the archetypal compromiser, the man despised by the prophets for 'halting between two opinions', and condemned for dithering until all is lost.

But is the contrast really as stark as this? When all has been said about the necessary element of absolutism in religion, and when the weakness of mere indecisiveness has been exposed, is there not a middle ground on which compromise can be seen as the expression of faith? What follows is an attempt to spell out the limits of this middle ground, in so far as they are affected by three theological considerations:

(1) Troeltsch made the point that a church-type Christianity can accept compromises far more readily than a sect-type. The ideal of the Kingdom of God 'requires a new world if it is to be fully

3   Nigel Balchin, *Lord I Was Afraid* (1947) p. 320.

realized . . .' but it 'cannot be realized within this world apart from compromise. Therefore the history of the Christian ethos becomes the story of a constantly renewed search for this compromise, and of fresh opposition to this spirit of compromise. The Church in particular, however, as a popular institution, is forced to compromise; this she effects by transferring to the institution the sanctity and the grace of forgiveness proper to it as an institution . . .'[4] In other words, the more the Church regards itself as possessing the objective treasures of grace, the less it need be damaged by the absence of personal holiness among its members, and the compromises into which it is forced by the pressure of events. The Church is holy, but its holiness is compatible with its role as a school for sinners, rather than a society for saints.

A sect, on the other hand, in its pure form tries to realize the ideal of the Kingdom of God with the fewest possible concessions to human frailty. It admits little room for compromise, and depends for its identity on the actual holiness of believers. It is therefore inevitably confined within strict limits, and pushed out of the mainstream of social life.

The notion that compromises can be tolerated within some sort of objective framework of grace, can usefully be linked with Reinhold Niebuhr's insistence that what he calls 'the paradox of grace' reveals the finiteness and sinfulness of all historical activities. Niebuhr would not, of course, have tolerated the idea of an 'objective framework of grace' somehow guaranteed by an institutional church, because any church, as part of history, falls under the same condemnation as every human endeavour, and is most to be condemned when its claims are greatest. But the context of grace, however received and known, allows and makes possible – indeed makes necessary – real admissions of ignorance, partiality and the distorting effects of sinful finite minds.

To live by grace is to have and not to have, because the having depends on God; it is to know and not to know; it is to act, and to admit the limitations of action, because only God can overcome the effects of human egotism. For Niebuhr one of the most disastrous mistakes Christians can make is to take the absolutist elements in Christian faith and translate them into programmes, and thus event-

4 Ernst Troeltsch, *The Social Teaching of the Christian Churches* (1931 edn), p. 999.

ually into fanaticisms. This is not to say that strong convictions should never be turned into effective actions. On the contrary, firm action, not least within the political realm, is essential. But to acknowledge the limitations of action, and to act within a spirit of forgiveness and an awareness of grace, is to be freed from the paralysis engendered by a sense of our own inadequacies; and freed also from the intolerance which refuses to take seriously the convictions of others.

Political action, thus understood, is inevitably marked by compromise. Neibuhr has harsh words for the kind of sectarian perfectionism which was 'blind to the inevitability of the compromises in which it saw its opponents involved. It therefore poured the fury of its self-righteous scorn upon them without recognizing that their compromises were but the obverse side of responsibilities, which the perfectionists had simply disavowed'.[5] Too much tolerance, on the other hand, too great a willingness to compromise, may merely reveal another kind of irresponsibility, indifference towards the problems of political justice.

It is not surprising that Niebuhr's careful balance, his unblinkered perception of sin, and his strong sense of the realities of power should have given him a dominant position in Christian political thinking. Since his day the trickle of Christian political comment has turned into a flood, and politicised theology has dug much deeper into the practical implications of translating gospel insights into political programmes. Christians who are prepared to get their hands dirty and to face the realities of political compromise, are much more common than they used to be. But Niebuhr's warnings still stand, and mark out the territory within which such activity can retain its Christian roots. The paradox of grace defines the relationship of human beings to God, and every other relationship must derive its Christian quality from this primary one.

(2) A second element in this attempt at map-making, defining the middle ground of faithful compromise, takes us back to the subject of religious language. The tendency, already mentioned, to push ideas and images to their limits is only one of its characteristics. Another is its obliqueness.[6]

---

5 Reinhold Niebuhr, *The Nature and Destiny of Man*, vol. II (1943), p. 242.
6 Tinsley, 'Tell It Slant' (1980).

Jesus spoke in parables. Straight answers to straight questions are rare in his teaching. His favourite method was to illuminate some problem by putting it in a fresh context, and then pass it back to the questioner. To reply to the question 'Who is my neighbour?' by telling the story of the Good Samaritan is to do more than provide a vivid illustration of some simple truth about neighbours being people in trouble. The story reverberates on many levels, and can be interpreted in many ways, and allows the hearer to identify himself with more than one character. There is a real sense, therefore, in which the hearer provides his own answer to the original question. An oblique shaft of light shows him where he stands and what he is. It helps to reveal God by conveying an awareness of multiple layers of meaning in which the hearer himself is involved.

Much communication between friends and lovers is indirect, allusive, only half-expressed. Its very inarticulateness can give it depth. It depends upon two people, not just on the speaker. To be addressed like a public meeting, as Queen Victoria discovered, is quite a different experience. So too God in communicating with us is present in the silences and reveals himself through the unspoken words. Obliqueness, far from being a disadvantage in religious discourse, may be the only way to express the inexpressible.

In St John's Gospel it takes the form of irony. The signs around which the story is constructed both reveal and conceal. They divide those who understand them from those who see only one level of meaning, and who express their incomprehension in words which themselves carry unrecognized overtones. When Pilate said of Jesus, 'Behold your king', the ironic reverberations were endless.

But there is another process also going on in St John's Gospel, which C. K. Barrett refers to as 'dialectic'.[7] Ideas and images are taken up, thrown about, looked at first from this side, then from that, argued against, reaffirmed and combined, in ways which make the reading of the Gospel a somewhat bewildering experience. To follow the ramifications of an apparently simple word like 'work', or an idea like that of 'coming to Jesus' through this text is to be taken up into a conversation rather than to be confronted by straight exposition.

It is at this point that the relevance of these sketchy observations

---

7   C. K. Barrett, *New Testament Essays* (1972), ch. 4: The Dialectical Theology of St John.

to the theme of compromise may begin to be apparent. If one of the modes of Biblical revelation is through the entry of its readers into a complex dialectical process in which they themselves are involved, then the notion, that somehow amid the confusions of life there always ought to be some single line of action which can be identified clearly and indubitably as 'the will of God', begins to look less convincing.

There are times when it is possible to be morally certain that one does indeed know the will of God, just as there are aspects of Christian teaching which are not oblique. The command to love one another may have endless implications; but it means just what it says. There are other times, however, when the idea that there must be some uniquely right solution to every complex problem leads either to a fruitless search for perfection, or to an intolerant defence of the chosen solution against every alternative. A God who reveals himself in hints and glimpses, who draws out a response from those engaged with him, must surely will that his creatures fulfil his purposes, not by one route, but by many.

In a sense this is so obvious that my excursion into Biblical exposition may seem an unnecessarily roundabout way of making a simple point. Yet the notion that the will of God must somehow be unequivocal exercises a curious fascination over Christian minds. It leads to the suspicion that the ordinary human processes of argumentation and bargaining which result in compromises, represent a falling away from the ideal. The inner voice whispering, 'This is the way; walk ye in it,' seems a more appropriate guide to the life of faith than the hard won conclusions of some committee. To acknowledge that obliqueness and dialectic may have their place in revelation, therefore, may help some Christians to place more value on their counterparts in ordinary life.

The acknowledgement must not be taken so far, though, as to evacuate the notion of the will of God of all content. Trying to discern the will of God is more than trying to come to a sensible compromise. Compromise, perhaps some unavoidable and agonizing choice between evils, may have a part in it. But the reference to the will of God, like all references to the transcendent, adds a new dimension to decision-making. It is a reminder of the imperfection of all merely human processes of willing. It sets limits to the inadequacy claimed for all merely human responses. Donald MacKinnon once wrote movingly of how 'a recollection of religious perspectives may restrain a man, in the sense of preventing him from seeing his choice as other than it is, as something which leaves many claims unacknowledged, that leaves him indeed with problems still to solve, claims however properly disregarded that he must yet somehow meet.'[8]

The faith which allows us to accept compromises for what they are, must also point beyond them. And this leads to a third consideration in the attempt to map out some Christian limits.

(3) Classical moral theology deals with compromise as the ultimate means of avoiding the choice between two evils. Personal morality was primarily in view, but the main principle elaborated seems to apply equally well to political choices. Compromise can be justified as a device for gaining time.

The essential context for justifiable compromise is that the evils envisaged in a straightforward and immediate choice must be equally unavoidable and undesirable. Moralists have sometimes gone to great lengths in trying to weigh values one against the other, and to work out some sort of balance sheet for the long- and short-term consequences of our actions. Such exercises have their place, whether they are done in traditional ethical terms or as some kind of cost/benefit analysis. But when, as often as not, no clear answer emerges, arbitrary choice or compromise may be the only alternatives left. 'A moral compromise, nobly undertaken and bravely endured', wrote Kirk, 'may enshrine a greater devotion of service and of faith than a reckless embracing of one alternative, even though the world calls the latter heroic and the former merely base.'[9] Only for a limited period, though.

Compromise, as Kirk understood it, is a device for deferring decisions to a more favourable time. It is not a settlement, but a staving off of the evil day in the hope that something else will turn up. In this respect it differs from the kind of statesmanlike compromise a politician might work for as a permanent means of resolving competing interests. When the context is a conflict between evils rather than between interests, compromise contains an element of connivance with evil, which is dangerous if it is allowed to continue unchecked, and eventually unnoticed. Such compromises harden

8   D. M. MacKinnon, *A Study in Ethical Theory* (1957), p. 264.
9   K. E. Kirk, *Conscience and its Problems* (1927), p. 374.

into solutions which embody the evils from which they were intended to provide the means of escape.

The emphasis on forbearance, on not pushing ahead with decisions recklessly in order to appear decisive, is the main positive factor in compromise according to this analysis. Its main negative factor is the peril of compliance and complacency.

In our day nuclear deterrence provides the most momentous example of a choice between evils. It is interesting to note how at the height of the original Campaign for Nuclear Disarmament the plea was made by responsible Christian bodies for more time. David Edwards, writing in 1963 as the spokesman of the group which developed into C.C.A.D.D. (Council on Christian Approaches to Defense and Disarmament) said . . . 'with a heavy heart I expect that nuclear weapons will remain in existence *for some years to come* . . .'[10] In the same year the British Council of Churches stated, 'The Council is convinced that these things are an offence to God and a denial of his purpose for man. Only the *rapid progressive reduction* of these weapons, their submission to strict international control and their eventual abolition can remove this offence.'[11] The implication is that a monstrosity can be tolerated for fear of something worse, but only if there is clear evidence that the compromise is a temporary one.

Twenty years later, despite limited gains, the nuclear powers remain as firmly committed as ever to the use of such weapons, and the dangers of their world-wide proliferation have increased. The sense that time is running out, that a moral enormity can be accepted only for so long and no longer, is one of the factors underlying the resurgence of anti-nuclear feeling. Though traditional moral theology contains plenty of warnings against impatience, the belief that we ought to be moving faster, and in the right direction, has a strong claim on the Christian conscience.

The time horizon within which decisions have to be made is a matter of increasing importance within the political sphere, for two reasons which work in opposition to one another. On the one hand, the availability of instant news on a worldwide scale, and the possibility of instant reactions to events, puts pressure on politicians to define their attitudes long before it may be strictly necessary for

10   D. L. Edwards, *Withdrawing from the Brink in 1963* (1963), p. 18.
11   Quoted in *The Future of the British Nuclear Deterrent* (B.C.C. 1979), p. iii.

them to do so. On the other hand, there is the fact that many of the processes on which the modern world depends have long lead times for their development and may call for decisions to be made many decades in advance. Energy policy is an obvious example. Politicians, therefore, find themselves caught between two time-scales, and because the immediate pressures are likely to be stronger than the more remote ones, far-reaching decisions are frequently postponed.

Here again an awareness of moral time-limits within which compromises are allowable, may help to define the border between cautious flexibility and weak-willed procrastination.

Theological reflections can do no more than touch the margins of the complex problems with which politicians have to wrestle. The quality of the answers found, however, may depend rather heavily on the way in which politicians themselves, and those whom they represent, understand the limitations within which they are operating. An acceptance of the paradox of grace, for instance, may give the moral courage needed to take some decisive action, without the arrogance which then refuses to admit that it might be wrong. A sense of the complex dialogue in which God engages with his people, may alert them to hitherto unrecognized voices in unexpected places. A recognition that God's infinite patience is held within the context of his ultimate judgement, may give a sense of urgency to seize the creative moment when it comes. An acknowledgement that some otherwise messy compromises may nevertheless be faithful, can help to reduce guilt and recrimination. And the admission that some may be unfaithful, is a necessary safeguard against the ever-present danger of self-deception.

Bibliography

BOOKS:

Adair, J., *The Becoming Church* (1977).

ARCIC, *The Final Report* (1982).

Balchin, N., *Lord, I was Afraid* (1947).

Barrett, C. K., *New Testament Essays* (1972).

Beeson, T., *The Church of England in Crisis* (1973).

Berger, P. L., *The Social Reality of Religion* (1969).

Berger, P. L., *A Rumour of Angels* (1969).

Berger, P. L., Berger, B. and Kellner, H., *The Homeless Mind* (1973).

Bowker, J., *The Sense of God* (1973).

Bowker, J., *The Religious Imagination and the Sense of God* (1978).

British Council of Churches, *The Future of the British Nuclear Deterrent* (1979).

British Council of Churches, *Towards Understanding the Arab/Israeli Conflict* (1982).

Budd, S., *Sociologists and Religion* (1973).

Bulmer, M., (ed.), *Working-Class Images of Society* (1975).

Chadwick, O., *The Secularization of the European Mind in the Nineteenth Century* (1975).

Chadwick Report, *Church and State* (1970).

Cornwall, P. R., *The Church and the Nation: The Case for Disestablishment* (1983).

Cowling, M., *Religion and Public Doctrine in Modern England* (1980).

Cox, H., *The Secular City* (1965).

Cupitt, D., *The Leap of Reason* (1976).

Currie, R., Gilbert, A. and Horsley, L., *Churches and Churchgoers: Patterns of Church Growth in the British Isles since 1700* (1977).

Dennis, N., *People and Planning* (1970).

Douglas, M., *Natural Symbols* (1970 Penguin edn.)

Dunne, J. S., *The City of the Gods* (1965).

Dunstan, G. R., *The Artifice of Ethics* (1974).

Edwards, D. L., *Withdrawing from the Brink in 1963* (1963).

Edwards, D. L., *Religion and Change* (1969).

Edwards, D. L., *The British Churches Turn to the Future* (1973).

Eliot, T. S., *The Idea of a Christian Society* (1939), also 1982 edition.

Emmet, D., *The Moral Prism* (1979).

191

Furlong, M., *Travelling In* (1971).

Gay, J. D., *The Geography of Religion in England* (1971).

Gilbert, A., *The Making of Post-Christian Britain* (1980).

Gill, R., *The Social Context of Theology* (1975).

Gill, R., *Theology and Social Structure* (1977).

Gill, R., *Prophecy and Praxis* (1981).

Glasner, P. E., *The Sociology of Secularization* (1977).

Goodwin, G. (ed.), *Ethics and Nuclear Deterrence* (1982).

Greeley, A. M., *Unsecular Man: The Persistence of Religion* (1972).

Habgood, J. S., *A Working Faith* (1980).

Halsey, A. H., *Change in British Society* (1981 edn).

Hampshire, S., (ed.), *Public and Private Morality* (1978).

Hanson, A. H. and Walles, M., *Governing Britain* (1980 edn).

Harries, R., (ed.), *What Hope in an Armed World?* (1982).

Henson, H. H., *Disestablishment* (1929).

Henson, H. H., *Bishoprick Papers* (1946).

Herberg, W., *Protestant, Catholic, Jew* (1960).

Hinchliff, P., *Holiness and Politics* (1982).

Hoggart, R., *The Uses of Literacy* (1957).

Jenkins, D., *The British: Their Identity and Their Religion* (1975).

Johnson, N., *In Search of the Constitution: Reflections on State and Society in Britain* (1976).

Kelvin, P., *The Bases of Social Behaviour* (1969).

Kirk, K. E., *Conscience and Its Problems* (1927).

Kitcher, P., *Abusing Science: The Case against Creationism* (1982).

Koyama, K., *Waterbuffalo Theology* (1974).

Laslett, P., (ed.), *Philosophy, Politics and Society* (1970).

Luckmann, T., *The Invisible Religion* (1967).

McCormick, R. A., *How Brave a New World?* (1981).

MacKinnon, D. M., *A Study in Ethical Theory* (1957).

Macmurray, J., *Persons in Relation* (1961).

Martin, D., *A Sociology of English Religion* (1967).

Martin, D., *A General Theory of Secularization* (1978).

Martin, D., *The Dilemmas of Contemporary Religion* (1978).

Martin, D., (ed.), *Sociology and Theology: Alliance and Conflict* (1980).

Martin, D., *The Breaking of the Image* (1980).

Martin, D. and Mullen, P., (eds.), *No Alternative: The Prayer Book Controversy* (1981).

Marwick, A., *British Society since 1945* (1982).

Mitchell, B., *Law, Morality and Religion in a Secular Society* (1967).

Munby, D. L., *The Idea of a Secular Society and Its Significance for Christians* (1963).

Nicholls, D., *The Pluralist State* (1975).

Niebuhr, Richard, *Christ and Culture* (1952).

Niebuhr, Reinhold, *The Nature and Destiny of Man* (1943).

Norman, E. R., *Church and Society in England 1770–1970* (1976).

Paul, L., *The Payment and Deployment of the Clergy* (1964).

Paul, L., *A Church by Daylight* (1973).

Perman, D., *Change and the Churches* (1977).
Powell, E., *Wrestling with the Angel* (1977).
Quinton, A., *The Politics of Imperfection* (1978).
Ramsey, I. T., *Religious Language* (1957).
Reed, B., *The Dynamics of Religion: Process and Movement in Christian Churches* (1978).
Richards, M., *The Church of Christ* (1983).
Russell, A., *The Clerical Profession* (1980).
Salisbury Report, *The Church and the Bomb* (1982).
Santer, M., (ed.), *Their Lord and Ours* (1982).
Schneider, L., (ed.), *Religion, Culture and Society* (1964).
Sheppard, D., *Built as a City* (1973).
Sheppard, D., *Bias to the Poor* (1983).
Sims, N. A., (ed.), *Explorations in Ethics and International Relations* (1981).
Sykes, S., *The Integrity of Anglicanism* (1978).
Thompson, K. A., *Bureaucracy and Church Reform* (1970).
Tillich, P., *The Dynamics of Faith* (1957).
Towler, R., *Homo Religiosus* (1974).
Towler, R. and Coxon, A. P. M., *The Fate of the Anglican Clergy* (1979).
Trigg, R., *The Shaping of Man* (1982).
Troeltsch, E., *The Social Teaching of the Christian Churches* (1931).
Turner, J. M., *Queen's Essays* (1980).
Vanstone, W. H., *Love's Endeavour Love's Expense* (1977).
Weber, M., *Essays in Sociology* (1958 edn.).
Wilkinson, A., *The Church of England and the First World War* (1978).
Williams, R., *The Truce of God* (1983).
Wilson, B., *Religion in Secular Society* (1966).
Wilson, E. O., *On Human Nature* (1978).
World Council of Churches, *Faith and Science in an Unjust World* (1980).
W.C.C., *Baptism, Eucharist and Ministry* (1982).
W.C.C., *Before It's Too Late: The Challenge of Nuclear Disarmament* (1982).
Ziman, J., *Reliable Knowledge: An Exploration of the Grounds for Belief in Science* (1978).

ARTICLES AND PAMPHLETS:
Bocock, R. J., 'Ritual: Civic and Religious', *British Journal of Sociology 21*, 285 (1970).
Brewster, K., 'Purpose in a Voluntary Society', *The Cambridge Review 103*, 327 (1982).
Church Information Office, *To a Rebellious House?* (1981).
Conway, M., *Through the Eyes of the Poor* (1980).
Cupitt, D., 'The Leap of Reason', *Theology* LXXVIII, 297 (1975).
Gilkey, L., 'The New Watershed in Theology,' *Soundings*, LXIV, 119 (1981).
Grundy, M., 'The Death of Secular Man', *Theology* LXXXII, 349 (1979).
Habgood, J. S., 'Directions for the Church of England', *Theology* LXXIX, 132 (1976).
Habgood, J. S., 'On Being a Liturgical Reviser', *Theology* LXXXII, 95 (1979).

Hammerton, A. and Downing, A. C., 'Fringe Belief among Undergraduates', *Theology* LXXXII, 433 (1979).

Homan, R., 'Theology and Sociology: A Plea for Sociological Freedom', *Theology* LXXXIV, 428 (1981).

Hunt, G., 'The Church: Two Points of View', *Theology* LXXXIII, 257 (1980).

Jenkins, D., 'The Impossibility and the Necessity of the Church', *Crucible* (1974), 108.

Lockwood, D., Review article on T. H. Marshall, *Sociology 8*, 365 (1974).

Moyser, G., 'Patterns of Representation in the Elections to the General Synod in 1975', *Crucible* (1979).

Moyser, G., 'The 1980 General Synod: Patterns and Trends', *Crucible* (1982).

Musgrove, F. and Middleton, R., 'Rites of Passage and the Meaning of Age in Three Contrasted Social Groups', *The British Journal of Sociology 32*, 39 (1981).

P.N. Review 13, 'Crisis for Cranmer and King James' (1979).

Preston, R. H., 'Secularization and Renewal', *Crucible* (1977), 68.

Ridley, B., 'Government and Leadership in the Church', *Theology* LXXXI, 190 (1978).

Song, C. S., 'Racism and the Unity of the Church', *PCR Information* (W.C.C.) 50 (1980).

Tinsley, J., 'Tell It Slant'. *Theology* LXXXIII, 163 (1980).

U.S. Episcopal Conference, *The Challenge of Peace: God's Promise and Our Response* (1983).

Visser 'T Hooft, W. A., 'Evangelism among Europe's Neo-Pagans', *International Review of Mission* (1977) 349.

Willmer, H., 'Forgiveness and Politics', *Crucible* (1979) 100.

World Council of Churches, 'Councils, Conciliarity and a Genuinely Universal Council', *W.C.C. Study Encounter* SE/57 (1974).

Name Index